the yarn girls' guide to
knits for all seasons

the yarn girls' guide to
knits for all seasons

Sweaters and Accessories for Men and Women

JULIE CARLES AND JORDANA JACOBS
photography by ellen silverman

POTTER
CRAFT

NEW YORK

Copyright © 2007
by Julie Carles and
Jordana Jacobs
Photography copyright
© 2007 by Ellen Silverman

Published in the United States
by Potter Craft, an imprint of
the Crown Publishing Group,
a division of Random House, Inc.,
New York.
www.crownpublishing.com
www.pottercraft.com

POTTER CRAFT and colophon
and POTTER and colophon are
registered trademarks of
Random House, Inc.

Library of Congress
Cataloging-in-Publication
Data

Carles, Julie
    The yarn girls' guide to knits for all
seasons sweaters and accessories for men
and women / Julie Carles and Jordana
Jacobs ; photography by Ellen Silverman.
    — 1st ed.
p.   cm.
  Includes index.
   ISBN: 978-0-307-34594-3
    1. Knitting—Patterns.   2. Sweaters.
   I. Jacobs, Jordana.   II. Title.
TT825.C1825   2007
746.43'20432—dc22   2006028122

ISBN 978-0-307-34594-3

Printed in China

Design by Jennifer K. Beal

10 9 8 7 6 5 4 3 2 1

First Edition

Dedicated to all the Yarn Co. loyal and inspiring customers.

Acknowledgments

We are very grateful to everyone who helped us with this book.

Thank you to the wonderful, beautiful, and handsome models who took time out of their busy schedules to bring life to the sweaters: Daniele Merlis, Wendy Struele, Christina Holmes, Nici McNally, Kristina Vincze (whose real job was as our fabulous makeup artist), Julien Yoo, Karyn Zieve, Tara Polius, John Carles, Jeff Jacobs, Seth Mayeri, and Jamison Dalton.

Our fabulous photographer, Ellen Silverman, who has a great eye.

Janine Lynch-Nerney, for the great styles she chose to coordinate with our knits.

Mercedes Bravo, for tirelessly and expertly knitting the sweaters.

Our dedicated and patient agent, Carla Glasser.

Daniella Tineo, for the clear schematic illustrations.

The Yarn Co. staff, for their dedication and hard work.

Contents

introduction

Knitting is not just a cold-weather activity anymore—it is a relaxing, meditative hobby that you can have fun doing in any type of weather. Although most people think of fall and winter as the true knitting seasons, there are great things to knit in the warmer weather, too. Great fibers and wonderful styles are just as accessible for spring and summer knitting. We decided to write this book, which divides the projects up into four chapters (one for each of the four seasons), in order to illustrate that knitting really and truly is a hobby for all seasons.

For spring we chose lighter fibers like cotton, linen, and rayon. The sweaters we designed are light, yet most provide a bit of warmth to keep the chill away. Others are for the warmer days of spring, when a T-shirt is just perfect.

Summer is all about wearing bright colors and light fibers—and not covering up too much. Tank tops, halters, cute skirts, and dresses make summer knitting fun. Colors that mirror the brightness of the summer months are an important part of summer knitting. Think flowers, bright blue skies, and cool tropical drinks.

For fall we chose styles that are fashionable yet comfy. The sweaters in the fall chapter are perfect for a brisk walk in the park on a clear, cool day, or they can be worn casually to work. We used fibers that are lightweight yet warm: soft and snuggly alpaca, fine merino wool, and kid mohair are perfect for fall weather. Color plays an important role in our fall chapter—autumnal hues like oranges, deep reds, burgundies, and greens radiate the essence of the season.

For winter we focused more on warmth, incorporating thicker yarns. Just because yarn is warm and thick does not mean it is itchy. These days yarn can be thick as well as light and soft. We used such fibers as yak, cashmere, and merino wool, all of which are soft, luxurious, and sure to keep you warm on even the coldest of days. We also included a few styles that reflect the cheer of the holiday season. Fur and a little shimmer make some simple styles a bit more festive.

This book differs from the others in our *Yarn Girls'* series in that it is strictly a book of patterns, with forty projects for you to knit. There is no how-to section or step-by-step guides aside from the finishing techniques in the back (page 152)—just projects, projects, and more projects. Each chapter includes ten patterns: six women's garments, two women's accessories, and two men's sweaters. The projects are all geared toward beginner to intermediate knitters. Many patterns are knit in simple stockinette stitch but include an interesting shape or detail. We also use some simple cables and stitches—but mostly the garments are about shapes and styles.

We are also happy to provide a total of eight men's patterns. There really is a scarcity of knitting patterns for men, so we tried to include a nice range of styles throughout the book. You'll find a cardigan, V-necks, a turtle-neck, a raglan pullover, a crew neck pullover, and even a saddle shoulder.

Finally, just a quick note about seasonal knitting: knitting seasons do not really begin when the true seasons do. Always try to be one step ahead—fall/winter yarns usually arrive in mid-summer, while spring/summer yarns tend to arrive in late winter. You can take advantage of this timing if you are not a super-speedy knitter by starting your projects for the next season early so that you can enjoy wearing them at the correct time of year.

We hope you enjoy the patterns in this book. We had fun coming up with them and hope they inspire you to try out new styles and fibers, whether you're at the pool or curled up on the couch during a snowstorm.

Julie & Jordana

knitting glossary

C2B Cable 2 into back. Slip 1 stitch to cable needle, hold at front, knit 1 stitch from left-hand needle, knit 1 from cable needle.

C2F Cable 2 into front. Slip 1 stitch to cable needle, hold at back, knit 1 stitch from left-hand needle, knit 1 from cable needle.

C3B Cable 3 into back. Slip 2 stitches onto cable needle, hold at back, knit 1 stitch from left-hand needle, knit 2 stitches from cable needle.

C3F Cable 3 into front. Slip 1 stitch onto cable needle, hold at front, knit 2 stitches from left-hand needle, knit 1 stitch from cable needle.

C6B Cable 6 into back. Slip 3 stitches to cable needle, hold at back, knit 3 stitches from left-hand needle, knit 3 stitches from cable needle.

CC Contrast color.

DEC Decrease.

GARTER STITCH Knit every row.

INC Increase.

K Knit.

K2TOG Knit 2 stitches together.

K3TOG Knit 3 stitches together.

MC Main color.

P Purl.

P2TOG Purl 2 stitches together.

P3TOG Purl 3 stitches together.

PM Place marker.

PSSO Pass slip stitch over.

RS Right side. This refers to the surface of the work that will face outside when you are wearing the garment.

SEED STITCH Worked over an odd number of stitches. K1, P1 every row. Worked over an even number of stitches—Row 1: K1, P1; Row 2: P1, K1.

SL Slip.

SSK Slip, slip, knit. Slip 2 stitches as if you were going to knit them (one at a time) to the right-hand needle. Insert the left-hand needle into the front of the 2 stitches and knit them together.

ST ST Stockinette stitch. Knit 1 row on the RS. Purl 1 row on the WS.

WS Wrong side. This refers to the surface of the work that will face inside when you are wearing it.

YO Yarn over.

spring

Despite all the pleasures it brings, spring is a tricky season. One day it's 70 degrees and sunny, the next it's damp, cold, and rainy. We think sweaters are the perfect way to to brave those Jekyll and Hyde days, and in this chapter we have provided you with all types of sweaters for all types of weather. For those early days of spring that are typically a little bit cool, we use silk/wool blends, merino wools, or thicker rayon ribbons and cottons. For the in-between days, we knit a cardigan in a chunky cotton/silk blend that breathes well and is easy to pull on and off again. And for those days when summer is teasing, we love lighter weight linen and cotton. Although we have chosen various fibers to accommodate the changes in weather, what the yarns in this chapter all have in common is that they are light-weight, soft, and comfortable against your skin.

nancy's knit

YARN: Alchemy, Syncronicity (110 yards/
50g ball)

FIBER CONTENT: 50% silk/50% wool

COLOR: Waterlily

AMOUNT: 9 (9, 10, 11) balls

TOTAL YARDAGE: 990 (990, 1100, 1210)
yards

GAUGE: 5³/₄ stitches = 1 inch; 23
stitches = 4 inches (in pattern)

NEEDLE SIZE: U.S. #7 (4.5mm) or size
needed to obtain gauge

SIZES: XS (S, M, L)

KNITTED MEASUREMENTS: Width =
16³/₄" (17³/₄", 18³/₄", 19³/₄"); Length = 21"
(21¹/₂", 22", 23"); Sleeve Length = 12¹/₂"
(13¹/₂", 14¹/₂", 15¹/₂")

Julie's mom, Nancy, who spends the summer out of Manhattan, called one day and said she needed a project and wanted Julie to pick something and send it to her. Well, Julie knew this was easier said than done, because Nancy is quite picky. A simple stockinette project would not do: Julie knew that it would be "too boring" for her mother. Since Nancy did not have a stitch book with her, Julie went through her books and found four stitches that Nancy could do without help. Julie sent the yarn and stitch patterns to Nancy. Nancy did a gauge with each pattern and decided that this diagonal rib was the perfect one for her. We created a pattern with a boat neck and three-quarter length sleeves to create horizontal lines that would contrast the diagonal rib. Julie went to visit her mother a few weeks later. She was so proud of her: the sweater was beautiful.

PATTERN STITCH:
(MULTIPLE OF 6 STITCHES)

ROW 1: *P3, K3; repeat from *.

ROW 2 (AND ALL EVEN ROWS): Knit the knit stitches and Purl the purl stitches.

ROW 3: P2, *K3, P3; repeat from *, end K3, P1.

ROW 5: P1, *K3, P3; repeat from *, end K3, P2.

ROW 7: *K3, P3; repeat from *.

ROW 9: K2, *P3, K3; repeat from *, end P3, K1.

ROW 11: K1, *P3, K3; repeat from *, end P3, K2.

ROW 12: See row 2.

BACK AND FRONT:

With #7 needle, cast on 96 (102, 108, 114) stitches. Work in pattern stitch until piece measures 13" (13¹/₂", 13¹/₂", 14") from the cast-on edge, ending with a WS row. SHAPE ARMHOLES: Bind off 4 stitches at the beginning of the next 2 rows. Bind off 3 stitches at the beginning of the following 2 rows. Bind off 2 stitches at the beginning of the following 2 rows. Then, decrease 1 stitch at each edge, every other row 2 (3, 3, 3) times until 74 (78, 84, 90)

stitches remain. Continue working in pattern stitch until piece measures 21" (21½", 22", 23") from cast-on edge, ending with a WS row. Bind off all stitches loosely.

SLEEVES:

With # 7 needle, cast on 54 (54, 60, 60) stitches and work in pattern stitch. **AT THE SAME TIME,** increase 1 stitch at each edge, every 6th row 12 (13, 11, 13) times until you have 78 (80, 82, 86) stitches. *Note: Increase leaving 2 edge stitches on either side. This means you should work 2 stitches, increase a stitch, work to the last 2 stitches, increase a stitch, and then work the remaining 2 stitches. Increasing like this makes it easier to sew up your seams.* Work until sleeve measures 12½" (13½", 14½", 15½") from cast-on edge, ending with a WS row. S H A P E   C A P: Bind off 4 stitches at the beginning of the next 2 rows. Bind off 3 stitches at the beginning of the following 2 rows. Bind off 2 stitches at the beginning of the following 2 rows. Then decrease 1 stitch at each edge, every other row 2 (3, 3, 3) times. Bind off 2 stitches at the beginning of the next 18 (18, 18, 20) rows until 20 (20, 22, 22) stitches remain. Bind off all stitches loosely.

Note: If you are unable to increase in pattern, it is perfectly fine to increase in stockinette.

FINISHING:

Sew shoulder seams together, leaving 9" in the center open for a neck. Sew sleeves on. Then sew up side and sleeve seams.

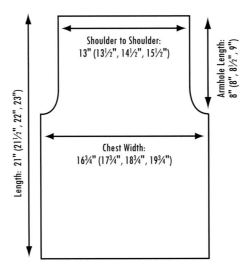

Shoulder to Shoulder:
13" (13½", 14½", 15½")

Armhole Length:
8" (8", 8½", 9")

Length: 21" (21½", 22", 23")

Chest Width:
16¾" (17¾", 18¾", 19¾")

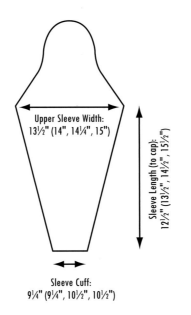

Upper Sleeve Width:
13½" (14", 14¼", 15")

Sleeve Length (to cap):
12½" (13½", 14½", 15½")

Sleeve Cuff:
9¼" (9¼", 10½", 10½")

knitting saves the day

YARN: Prism, Diana (55 yards/50g ball)

FIBER CONTENT: 100% rayon

COLOR: Tropicana

AMOUNT: 12 (13, 14, 15) balls

TOTAL YARDAGE: 660 (715, 770, 825) yards

STITCH GAUGE: 3¼ stitches = 1 inch; 13 stitches = 4 inches

ROW GAUGE: 4½ rows = 1 inch; 18 rows = 4 inches

NEEDLE SIZE: U.S. #11 (8mm) or size needed to obtain gauge; K (6.5mm) crochet hook

SIZES: XS (S, M, L)

KNITTED MEASUREMENTS: Width = 16" (17", 18½", 19"); Length = 20" (20½", 21", 21¾"); Sleeve Length = 16½" (17½", 18", 19")

Knitting cured Debbie of shopaholism. She is young and single and works 9 to 6 during the week and has all weekend to play. She used to spend most of her free time shopping because she loves clothes and fashion and didn't have much else to do. One day she came home from a day of shopping and realized she had no room for her new clothes. And then there was the matter of her credit card bills. She decided she needed a new hobby, and her friend suggested knitting. She took a class and knit a few scarves in a matter of weeks; then, she was ready to start a sweater. Since she was fashion savvy, she sketched out a simple design with raglan armholes and bell sleeves, and we wrote her the pattern with elegant and easy sleeves. We suggested a chunky rayon ribbon—which is actually a natural fiber—because it has great drape. It looked something like this...

BACK AND FRONT:

With #11 needle, cast on 52 (56, 60, 62) stitches. Work in St st until piece measures 12½" (12½", 12½", 13") from cast-on edge, ending with a WS row.

SHAPE RAGLAN ARMHOLES: Bind off 2 stitches at the beginning of the next 2 rows. Then decrease as follows: **ROW 1:** K2, SSK, knit to end. **ROW 2:** P2, P2tog, purl to end. **ROW 3:** Knit. **ROW 4:** Purl. Work rows 1–4 2 (3, 2, 2) more times until 42 (44, 50, 52) stitches remain. Then work rows 1 and 2 12 (11, 14, 15) times until 18 (22, 22, 22) stitches remain. Bind off all stitches loosely.

SLEEVES:

With #11 needle, cast on 40 (42, 46, 48) stitches. Work in St st until sleeve measures 16½" (17½", 18", 19") from cast-on edge, ending with a WS row. S H A P E R A G L A N S L E E V E : Bind off 2 stitches at the beginning of the next 2 rows. Then decrease as follows: **ROW 1:** K2, SSK, knit to end. **ROW 2:** P2, P2tog, purl to end. **ROW 3:** Knit. **ROW 4:** Purl. Work rows 1–4 2 (3, 2, 2) more times until 30 (30, 36, 38) stitches remain. Then work rows 1 and 2 12 (11, 14, 15) times until 6 (8, 8, 8) stitches remain. Bind off all stitches loosely.

FINISHING:

Sew raglan pieces together. With a K crochet hook, work 1 row single crochet around all edges.

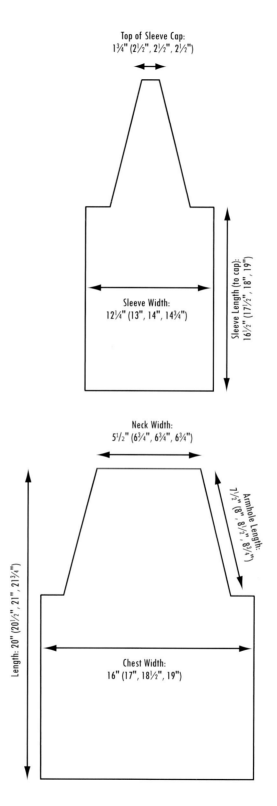

Top of Sleeve Cap:
1¾" (2½", 2½", 2½")

Sleeve Width:
12¼" (13", 14", 14¾")

Sleeve Length (to cap):
16½" (17½", 18", 19")

Neck Width:
5½" (6¾", 6¾", 6¾")

Armhole Length:
7½" (8", 8½", 8¾")

Length: 20" (20½", 21", 21¾")

Chest Width:
16" (17", 18½", 19")

knit 'n' talk

YARN: Lang, Columbo (55 yards/50g ball)

FIBER CONTENT: 53% silk/47% cotton

COLOR: 60

AMOUNT: 16 (17, 18, 20) balls

TOTAL YARDAGE: 880 (935, 990, 1100) yards

GAUGE: 3³/₄ stitches = 1 inch; 15 stitches = 4 inches (in pattern)

NEEDLE SIZE: U.S. #10¹/₂ (7mm) for body or size needed to obtain gauge; U.S. #9 (5.5mm) for ribbing

SIZES: XS (S, M, L)

KNITTED MEASUREMENTS: Width = 16¹/₂" (17¹/₂", 18¹/₂", 19³/₄"); Length = 21" (21¹/₂", 22", 23"); Sleeve Length = 16¹/₂" (17¹/₂", 18", 19")

OTHER MATERIALS: 5 buttons

Before she met her boyfriend, Lana had always knit very intricate cabled sweaters. Sitting down with some music and a challenging knitting pattern took her mind off her day's worries and stresses. She also loved the look of cables. But then she met Cliff. At night they would sit and talk and listen to music. After a few weeks of this, Lana realized she really missed knitting but she could not carry on an in-depth conversation while knitting the intricate patterns she was used to. So she came in to see us to see if we had some sort of solution. Jordana suggested this very simple cable pattern, which looks intricate because there are many cables close together. We chose a silk/cotton yarn to keep this four-row cabled cardigan lightweight. Lana decided to try it, and it worked great. She was finally able to knit and talk.

PATTERN STITCH: (MULTIPLES OF 4 STITCHES + 2)

C2B (cable 2 into back): Slip 1 stitch to cable needle, hold at back, knit 1 stitch from left-hand needle, knit 1 from cable needle.

ROW 1: *P2, C2B* end P2.

ROW 2: *K2, P2* end K2.

ROW 3: *P2, K2* end P2.

ROW 4: *K2, P2* end K2.

BACK:

With #9 needle, cast on 62 (66, 70, 74) stitches. Work in K1, P1 ribbing for 6 rows. Change to #10¹/₂ needles and work in pattern stitch until piece measures 13" (13¹/₄", 13¹/₂", 14") from cast-on edge, ending with a WS row. SHAPE ARMHOLES: Bind off 3 stitches at the beginning of the next 2 rows. Bind off 2 stitches at the beginning of the next 2 rows. Then decrease 1 stitch at each edge, every other row 2 (3, 4, 4) times until 48 (50, 52, 56) stitches remain. Continue to work in pattern stitch until piece measures 21" (21¹/₂", 22", 23") from cast-on edge, ending with a WS row. Bind off all stitches loosely.

FRONT: (MAKE 2, REVERSE SHAPING)

With #9 needle, cast on 30 (34, 34, 38) stitches. Work in K1, P1 ribbing for 6

rows. Change to #10½ needles and work in pattern stitch until piece measures 13" (13¼", 13½", 14") from cast-on edge, ending with a WS row for the left front and a RS row for the right front. SHAPE ARMHOLES AS FOR BACK AT SIDE EDGE ONLY until 23 (26, 25, 29) stitches remain. Continue to work in pattern stitch until piece measures 18½" (19", 19½", 20½") from cast-on edge, ending with a RS row for the left front and a WS row for the right front. SHAPE CREW NECK: At beginning of neck edge every other row, bind off 4 stitches 1 time, 3 stitches 1 time, 2 stitches 1 time, 1 stitch 2 (2, 2, 4) times. Continue to work in St st on remaining 12 (15, 14, 16) stitches until piece measures 21" (21½", 22", 23") from cast-on edge ending with a WS row. Bind off all stitches loosely.

SLEEVES:

With #9 needle, cast on 30 (30, 34, 34) stitches. Work in K1, P1 ribbing for 6 rows. Change to #10½ needle and work in pattern stitch. **AT THE SAME TIME,** increase 1 stitch at each edge, every 6th row 8 (10, 9, 11) times until you have 46 (50, 52, 56) stitches. *Note: Increase leaving 2 edge stitches on either side. This means you should work 2 stitches, increase a stitch, work to the last 2 stitches, increase a stitch, and then work the remaining 2 stitches. Increasing like this makes it easier to sew up your seams.* Work until sleeve measures 16½" (17½", 18", 19") from cast-on edge, ending with a WS row. SHAPE CAP: Bind off 3 stitches at the beginning of the next 2 rows. Bind off 2 stitches at the beginning of the next 2 rows. Then decrease 1 stitch at each edge, every other row 2 (3, 4, 4) times. Bind off 2 stitches at the beginning of the next 10 (10, 10, 12) rows until 12 (14, 14, 14) stitches remain. Bind off all stitches loosely.

FINISHING:

Sew shoulder seams together. Sew sleeves on. Sew up side and sleeve seams. With #9 needle and RS of right front neck facing you, pick up 58 (58, 58, 60) around neck. Work 6 rows in K1, P1 ribbing. Bind off all stitches loosely. BUTTON BAND (LEFT SIDE AS WORN): With #9 needle and RS facing you, pick up 80 (82, 84, 88) stitches. Work in K1, P1 ribbing for 6 rows. Bind off all stitches loosely. BUTTONHOLE BAND (RIGHT SIDE AS WORN): With #9 needle and RS facing you, pick up 80 (82, 84, 88) stitches. Work in K1, P1 ribbing for 3 rows. On 4th row, make buttonholes as follows: Rib 3 (2, 3, 3) *YO, Rib 2tog, Rib 16 (17, 17, 18)* repeat from * to * 3 more times, end YO, Rib 2tog, Rib 3 (2, 3, 3). Work in K1, P1 ribbing for 2 more rows. Bind off all stitches loosely. Sew on buttons.

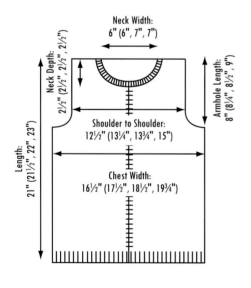

Neck Width: 6" (6", 7", 7")

Neck Depth: 2½" (2½", 2½", 2½")

Armhole Length: 8" (8¼", 8½", 9")

Length: 21" (21½", 22", 23")

Shoulder to Shoulder: 12½" (13¼", 13¾", 15")

Chest Width: 16½" (17½", 18½", 19¾")

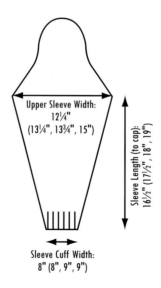

Upper Sleeve Width: 12¼" (13¼", 13¾", 15")

Sleeve Length (to cap): 16½" (17½", 18", 19")

Sleeve Cuff Width: 8" (8", 9", 9")

a work in progress

YARN: Tahki, Willow (81 yards/50g ball)

FIBER CONTENT: 66% linen/ 34% cotton

COLOR: 5003

AMOUNT: 6 (7, 8, 9) balls

TOTAL YARDAGE: 486 (567, 648, 729) yards

GAUGE: 4½ stitches = 1 inch; 18 stitches = 4 inches

NEEDLE SIZE: U.S. #8 (5mm) or size needed to obtain gauge, circular 16" U.S. #8 (5mm) for arm bands

SIZES: XS (S, M, L)

KNITTED MEASUREMENTS: Width = 16" (17", 18", 19"); Length = 21" (21½", 22", 23")

When we receive a new yarn, sometimes we start knitting it without an end product in mind. If we like the yarn, we do a gauge, cast on for a certain measurement, let our instincts go to work, and hope we end up with something we like. That's what happened with this sweater. Julie was knitting away. She had knit a back of a sweater in stockinette but decided to change the front a bit by knitting stockinette on the sides and reverse stockinette down the middle. She did not really have a pattern for, or an idea of, a finished neckline—it was a work in progress—and she figured she would know how to proceed as she kept knitting. When she got to the neck shaping, she decided on a high crew neck. She sewed the sweater together and edged the armholes. After trying it on, she liked it but felt something was missing. She had a few balls left, so the idea of a hood popped into her head. She figured it was worth a try. She knit it, sewed it on, and loved it.

BACK:

With #8 needle, cast on 72 (76, 82, 86) stitches. Work in garter stitch for 6 rows. Work in St st until piece measures 14½" (14½", 14½", 15") from the cast-on edge, ending with a WS row. SHAPE ARMHOLES: Bind off 4 stitches at the beginning of the next 2 rows. Bind off 3 stitches at the beginning of the following 2 rows. Bind off 2 stitches at the beginning of the following 2 rows. Then decrease 1 stitch at each edge, every other row 2 (3, 5, 4) times until 50 (52, 54, 60) stitches remain. Continue working in St st until piece measures 21" (21½", 22", 23") from cast-on edge, ending with a WS row. Bind off all stitches loosely.

FRONT:

With #8 needle, cast on 72 (76, 82, 86) stitches. Work in garter stitch for 6 rows. Then work in pattern as follows:

XS:

ROW 1: (RS) K26, P20, K26.

ROW 2: (WS) P26, K20, P26.

S:

ROW 1: (RS) K28, P20, K28.

ROW 2: (WS) P28, K20, P28.

M:

ROW 1: (RS) K29, P24, K29.

ROW 2: (WS) P29, K24, P29.

L:

ROW 1: (RS) K30, P26, K30.

ROW 2: (WS) P30, K26, P30.

Work until piece measures 14½" (14½", 14½", 15") from the cast-on edge, ending with a WS row. SHAPE ARM-HOLES: Bind off 4 stitches at the beginning of the next 2 rows. Bind off 3 stitches at the beginning of the following 2 rows. Bind off 2 stitches at the beginning of the following 2 rows. Then decrease 1 stitch at each edge, every other row 2 (3, 5, 4) times until 50 (52, 54, 60) stitches remain. Continue working in established pattern, making sure you keep the center 20 (20, 24, 26) stitches in purl on the RS and knit on the WS, until piece measures 18" (18½", 19", 20") from cast-on edge, ending with a WS row. SHAPE NECK: Bind off center 14 stitches and then begin working each side of the neck separately. At the beginning of each neck edge, every other row bind off 3 stitches 1 time, 2 stitches 1 time, and 1 stitch 3 (3, 4, 4) times. Continue to work on remaining 10 (11, 11, 14) stitches with no further decreasing until piece measures 21" (21½", 22", 23") from cast-on edge, ending with a WS row. Bind off all stitches loosely.

HOOD:

With #8 needle, cast on 40 (40, 42, 42) stitches. Work as follows: (RS) Knit. (WS) Purl to last 5 stitches, knit 5. Work until piece measures 23" (23", 24", 24").

FINISHING:

Sew shoulder seams together. Sew up sides. Sew back seam of hood. Sew on hood. With a 16" #8 circular needle pick up 68 (72, 76, 80) stitches around armholes. Work 6 rows garter stitch. Bind off all stitches loosely.

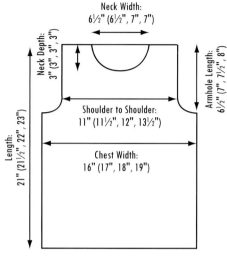

Neck Width:
6½" (6½", 7", 7")

Neck Depth:
3" (3", 3", 3")

Armhole Length:
6½" (7", 7½", 8")

Shoulder to Shoulder:
11" (11½", 12", 13½")

Chest Width:
16" (17", 18", 19")

Length:
21" (21½", 22", 23")

maximum wearability

YARN: Louet Sales, Euroflax (270 yards/100g ball)

FIBER CONTENT: 100% linen

COLORS: A: grape; B: eggplant

AMOUNT: A: 1 (1, 1, 1); B: 4 (4, 4, 5) balls

TOTAL YARDAGE: A: 270 (270, 270, 270); B: 1080 (1080, 1080, 1350) yards

GAUGE: 3½ stitches = 1 inch; 14 stitches = 4 inches

NEEDLE SIZE: U.S. #11 (8mm) or size needed to obtain gauge; K (6.5mm) crochet hook

SIZES: XS (S, M, L)

KNITTED MEASUREMENTS: Width = 16½" (17½", 19", 21"); Length = 21" (21½", 22", 23"); Sleeve Length = 16½" (17½", 18", 19")

Yarn is worked double throughout the sweater—this means you should hold 2 strands of yarn together as if they were 1.

Christina was on a tight budget, but she loved to knit with luxurious yarns. So when she knit a sweater she had to make sure that it was a style that she could wear with all sorts of outfits. She needed to "maximize its wearability," she told us. "I need to be able to wear it with a flowy skirt, cute capris, and beat up old jeans." We thought a loose-fitting V-neck sweater would be a good style and then decided to add a contrasting color to the sleeve bottoms for a little bit of interest. Christina chose a beautiful linen yarn with which to knit the sweater—perfect for any type of spring day—and doubled the yarn in order to minimize her knitting time.

BACK:

With #11 needle and 2 strands of **color B,** cast on 58 (62, 66, 74) stitches. Work in St st until piece measures 13" (13", 13½", 14") from cast-on edge, ending with a WS row. SHAPE ARMHOLES: Bind off 3 stitches at the beginning of the next 2 rows. Bind off 2 stitches at the beginning of the next 2 rows. Then decrease 1 stitch at each edge, every other row 1 (2, 2, 5) time(s) until 46 (48, 52, 54) stitches remain. Continue working in St st until piece measures 21" (21½", 22", 23) from cast-on edge, ending with a WS row. Bind off all stitches loosely.

FRONT:

With #11 needle and 2 strands of **color B,** cast on 58 (62, 66, 74) stitches. Work in St st until piece measures 13" (13", 13½", 14") from cast-on edge, ending with a WS row. SHAPE ARMHOLES: Bind off 3 stitches at the beginning of the next 2 rows. Bind off 2 stitches at the beginning of the next 2 rows. Then decrease 1 stitch at each edge, every other row 1 (2, 2, 5) time(s) until 46 (48, 52, 54) stitches remain. Continue working in St st until piece measures 14½" (14½", 14½", 15") from cast-on edge, ending with a WS row. SHAPE V-NECK: Place a marker at the center. ROW 1: Knit until 4 stitches before the marker, K2tog, K2. Turn work around as if you were at the end of the row. Ignore the rest of the stitches. ROW 2: Purl to end of row. ROW 3: Knit. ROW 4: Purl. Repeat rows 1–4 2 (2, 3, 4) more times until 20 (21, 22, 22) stitches remain. Then repeat rows 1 and 2 9 (10, 9, 9) times until 11 (11, 13, 13) stitches remain. Continue to work on these stitches until piece measures 21" (21½", 22", 23") from cast-on edge, ending with a WS row. Bind off remaining stitches loosely. Attach yarn to other side. You should be on a RS row. ROW 1: K2, SSK, knit until end. ROW 2: Purl. ROW 3: Knit. ROW 4: Purl. Repeat rows 1–4 2 (2, 3, 4) more times until 20 (21, 22, 22) stitches remain. Then repeat rows 1 and 2 9 (10,

9, 9) times until 11 (11, 13, 13) stitches remain. Continue to work on these stitches until piece measures 21" (21½", 22", 23") from cast-on edge, ending with a WS row. Bind off remaining stitches loosely.

SLEEVES:

With #11 needle and 2 strands of **color A,** cast on 28 (30, 32, 34) stitches. Work in St st until piece measures 6" (7", 7½", 8") from cast on edge ending with a WS row and change to 2 strands of **color B. AT THE SAME TIME,** increase 1 stitch at each edge, every 6th (6th, 8th, 8th) row 9 times until you have 46 (48, 50, 52) stitches. *Note: Increase leaving 2 edge stitches on either side of work. This means you should knit 2 stitches, increase a stitch, knit to the last 2 stitches, increase a stitch, and then knit the remaining 2 stitches. Increasing like this makes it easier to sew up your seams.* Continue in St st until sleeve measures 16½" (17½", 18", 19") from cast-on edge, ending with a WS row. S H A P E C A P : Bind off 3 stitches at the beginning of the next 2 rows. Bind off 2 stitches at the beginning of the next 2 rows. Then decrease 1 stitch at each edge, every other row 1 (2, 2, 5) time(s). Bind off 2 stitches at the beginning of the next 10 (10, 12, 10) rows. Bind off remaining 14 (14, 12, 12) stitches loosely.

FINISHING:

Sew shoulder seams together. Sew sleeves on and then sew down side and sleeve seams. With a K crochet hook work 1 row of single crochet around neck edge.

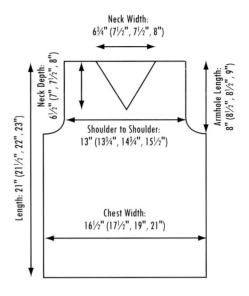

Neck Width:
6¾" (7½", 7½", 8")

Neck Depth:
6½" (7", 7½", 8")

Length: 21" (21½", 22", 23")

Armhole Length:
8" (8½", 8½", 9")

Shoulder to Shoulder:
13" (13¾", 14¾", 15½")

Chest Width:
16½" (17½", 19", 21")

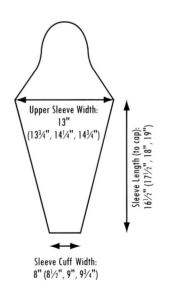

Upper Sleeve Width:
13"
(13¾", 14¼", 14¾")

Sleeve Length (to cap):
16½" (17½", 18", 19")

Sleeve Cuff Width:
8" (8½", 9", 9¾")

the rugby team

YARN: On Line, Clip (175 yards/ 100g ball)

FIBER CONTENT: 100% cotton

COLORS: A: 146; B: 20; C: white

AMOUNT: A and B: 2 (2, 2, 3); C: 1 (1, 1, 1) ball(s)

TOTAL YARDAGE: A and B: 350 (350, 350, 525); C: 175 (175, 175, 175) yards

GAUGE: 5 stitches = 1 inch; 20 stitches = 4 inches

NEEDLE SIZE: U.S. #6 (4mm) for body or size needed to obtain gauge; U.S. #4 (3.5mm) for ribbing

SIZES: XS (S, M, L)

KNITTED MEASUREMENTS: Width = 16" (17", 18", 19"); Length =22" (22$\frac{1}{2}$", 23", 23$\frac{1}{2}$"); Sleeve Length = 2$\frac{1}{2}$" (3", 3$\frac{1}{2}$", 4")

We went to University of Vermont, where rugby was a popular fall sport. Saturday afternoons were spent at rugby games hanging out with friends and a keg of beer. Fast forward about twenty years, and we were sitting around looking at old college pictures when we came across some from a rugby game we attended. After reminiscing about how cute the guys were, we started noticing that the shirts they were wearing were cute, too. A lot of the guys cut the sleeves above the elbow. We decided it would be a perfect cotton sweater for a woman, but it needed some feminizing. In addition to the simple stripe pattern and placket that are the signature of a rugby shirt, we added a frilly neck and short cap sleeves. Even after all these years, going to college is still paying off.

STRIPE PATTERN:

14 rows St st in **color A.**
14 rows St st in **color B.**

BACK:

With #4 needle and **color A,** cast on 80 (86, 90, 96) stitches. Work in K1, P1 ribbing for 6 rows. Change to #6 needle and work in St st stripe pattern until piece measures 14$\frac{1}{2}$" (14$\frac{1}{2}$", 14$\frac{1}{2}$", 14$\frac{1}{2}$") from the cast-on edge, ending with a WS row. SHAPE ARM-HOLES: Bind off 3 stitches at the beginning of the next 2 rows. Bind off 2 stitches at the beginning of the following 2 rows. Then decrease 1 stitch at each edge, every other row 4 (5, 5, 5) times until 62 (66, 70, 76) stitches remain. Continue working in St st stripe pattern until piece measures 22" (22$\frac{1}{2}$", 23", 23$\frac{1}{2}$") from cast-on edge, ending with a WS row. Bind off all stitches loosely.

FRONT:

With #4 needle and **color A,** cast on 80 (86, 90, 96) stitches. Work in K1, P1 ribbing for 6 rows. Change to #6 needle and work in St st stripe pattern until piece measures 14$\frac{1}{2}$" (14$\frac{1}{2}$", 14$\frac{1}{2}$", 14$\frac{1}{2}$") from the cast-on edge, ending with a WS row. SHAPE ARM-HOLES: Bind off 3 stitches at the beginning of the next 2 rows. Bind off 2 stitches at the beginning of the following 2 rows. Then decrease 1 stitch at each edge, every other row 4 (5, 5, 5) times until 62 (66, 70, 76) stitches remain. Continue working in St st stripe pattern until piece measures 16" (16$\frac{1}{2}$", 16$\frac{1}{2}$", 16$\frac{1}{2}$") from cast-on edge, ending

with a WS row. SHAPE PLACKET: Bind off center 4 stitches and then work each side of the neck separately in St st stripe pattern until piece measures 19$\frac{1}{2}$" (20", 20$\frac{1}{2}$", 21") from cast-on edge, ending with a WS row for right front and a RS row for left front. At the beginning of each neck edge every other row, bind off 4 stitches 1 time, 3 stitches 1 time, 2 stitches 1 time, and 1 stitch 3 (3, 3, 4) times. Continue to work on remaining 17 (19, 21, 23) stitches in St st stripe pattern with no further decreasing until piece measures 22" (22$\frac{1}{2}$", 23", 23$\frac{1}{2}$") from cast-on edge, ending with a WS row. Bind off all stitches loosely.

SLEEVES:

With #4 needle and **color A,** cast on 56 (58, 62, 66) stitches. Work in K1, P1 ribbing for 6 rows. Change to #6 needle and work in St st stripe pattern. **AT THE SAME TIME,** increase 1 stitch at each edge, every other row 3 (4, 4, 5) times until you have 62 (66, 70, 76) stitches. *Note: Increase leaving 2 edge stitches on either side. This means you should knit 2 stitches, increase a stitch, knit to the last 2 stitches, increase a stitch, and then knit the remaining 2 stitches. Increasing like this makes it easier to sew up your seams.* Work until sleeve measures 2$\frac{1}{2}$" (3", 3$\frac{1}{2}$", 4") from cast-on edge, ending with a WS row. SHAPE CAP: Bind off 3 stitches at the beginning of the next 2 rows. Bind off 2 stitches at the beginning of the following 2 rows. Then decrease 1 stitch at each edge, every other row 4 (5, 5, 5) times. Bind off 2 stitches at the beginning of the next 16 (16, 18, 20) rows until 12 (14, 14, 16) stitches remain. Bind off all stitches loosely.

FINISHING:

Sew shoulder seams together. Sew sleeves on. Then sew up side and sleeve seams. With #4 needle, **color C,** and right side facing, pick up 22 (22, 24, 26) stitches up on left placket. Work in K1, P1 ribbing for 7 rows. Bind off all stitches loosely. With #4 needle, **color C,** and right side facing, pick up 22 (22, 24, 26) stitches up on right placket. Work in K1, P1 ribbing for 3 rows. **BUTTONHOLE ROW:** Rib 4 (4, 5, 6), YO, Rib 2tog, Rib 10 (10, 10, 10), end YO, Rib 2tog, Rib 4 (4, 5, 6). Work 3 more rows in K1, P1 ribbing. Bind off all stitches loosely. With #4 needle, **color C,** and right side facing, pick up 85 (85, 85, 88) stitches around neck and work in K1, P1 ribbing for 2 rows. For XS, S, and M work **ROW 1:** K1, P1. **ROW 2:** P1, K1. For L: K1, P1 every row. **BUTTONHOLE ROW:** K1, P1 until last 5 stitches, Rib 2tog, YO, Rib 3. Work K1, P1 ribbing for 3 more rows. **AT THE SAME TIME,** on row 5 and row 6 bind off the first 5 stitches. You will have 75 (75, 75, 78) stitches. Continue to work in St st beginning with a knit row as follows: K2, knit into the front and back of each stitch across row until 2 stitches remain, K2. You will have 146 (146, 146, 152) stitches. Work in St st for 9 rows. Then work as follows: *K3, knit into the front and back of the next stitch* repeat from * to * until 2 (2, 2, 4) stitches remain, K2 (K2, K2, K4). You will have 182 (182, 182, 189) stitches. Bind off all stitches loosely.

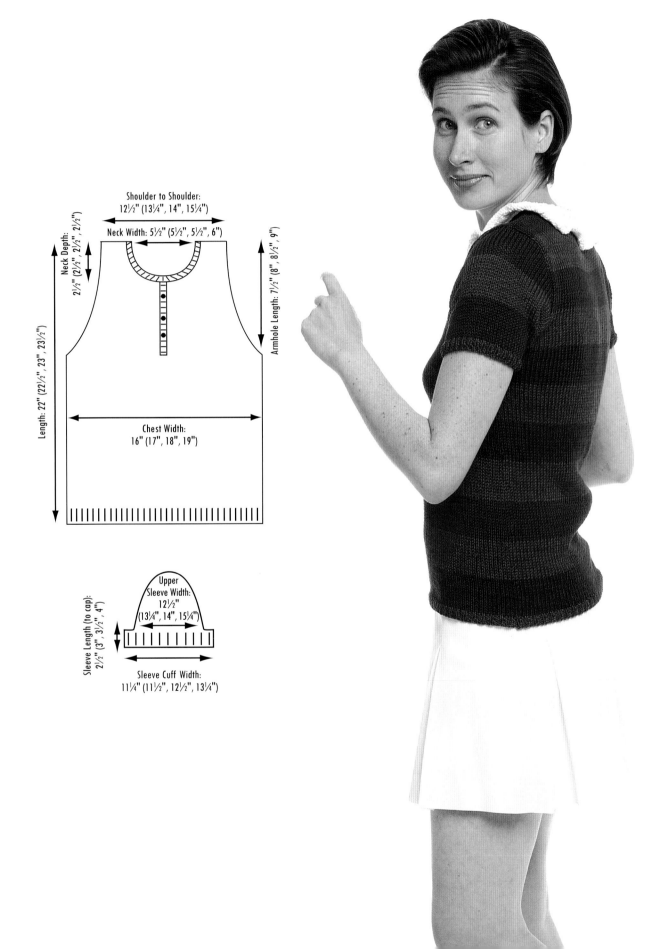

Shoulder to Shoulder:
12½" (13¼", 14", 15¼")

Neck Width: 5½" (5½", 5½", 6")

Neck Depth:
2½" (2½", 2½", 2½")

Armhole Length: 7½" (8", 8½", 9")

Length: 22" (22½", 23", 23½")

Chest Width:
16" (17", 18", 19")

Upper
Sleeve Width:
12½"
(13¼", 14", 15¼")

Sleeve Length (to cap):
2½" (3", 3½", 4")

Sleeve Cuff Width:
11¼" (11½", 12½", 13¼")

keep your pants on

YARN: Berroco, Suede (120 yards/50g ball)

FIBER CONTENT: 100% nylon

COLORS: Blue: 3704, red: 3719, green: 3715

AMOUNT: 1 ball

TOTAL YARDAGE: 120 yards

GAUGE: 5 stitches = 1 inch; 20 stitches = 4 inches

NEEDLE SIZE: U.S. #6 (4mm) or size needed to obtain gauge

SIZES: One size

KNITTED MEASUREMENTS: Width = 2"; Length = desired

Jane (names have been changed to protect identity), an avid knitter, was on a diet and losing weight left and right. Every time she came in, she'd constantly be pulling up her pants. She couldn't wear her belts because they were too big, and she refused to buy new clothes until she lost those last five pounds. One day, as her pants were riding too low, we suggested she knit a simple garter stitch belt that she could tie. She loved the idea and made several. Now, she is at her goal weight but can still wear these light, colorful belts.

BELT:

With #6 needle, cast on 10 stitches. Work in garter stitch until desired length.

FINISHING:

Cut 30 20" lengths of yarn. Using 3 strands of yarn per fringe, attach 5 fringes to each end.

for hairy weather

YARN: Filatura di Crosa, Millefili Fine (136 yards/50g ball)

FIBER CONTENT: 100% cotton

COLORS: A: 195 (red); B: 167 (tangerine); C: 286 (acid green); D: 272 (hot pink)

AMOUNT: 1 ball each A, B, C & D

TOTAL YARDAGE: 544 yards

GAUGE: 8 stitches = 1 inch; 32 stitches = 4 inches

NEEDLE SIZE: U.S. #3 (3mm) or size needed to obtain gauge; E (3.5mm) crochet hook

SIZES: One size

KNITTED MEASUREMENTS: Width = 2¹/₂"; Length = desired

Spring in the Northeast brings all sorts of weather. One day is sunny and 65 degrees, the next day is windy and rainy and 45 degrees. You can get any combination. One certainty is that hair whipping your face is not comfortable. Since spring is a time when you want to infuse color into your life, we thought this fun, useful, and colorful headband would be a perfect project.

PATTERN STITCH:

ROW 1 (RS): Using **color A,** Knit.

ROW 2: Using A, Purl.

ROW 3: Using **color B,** K2 *sl 4, K2; repeat from * to end.

ROW 4: Using B, P3, sl 2, *P4, sl 2; rep from * to last 3 sts, P3.

ROW 5: Using B, same as row 1.

ROW 6: Using B, same as row 2.

ROW 7: Using **color C,** K1, sl 2, K2, *sl 4, K2; rep from * to last 3 sts, sl 2, K1.

ROW 8: Using C, P1, sl 1, P4, * sl 2, P4; rep from * to last 2 sts, sl 1, P1.

ROW 9: Using C, same as row 1.

ROW 10: Using C, same as row 2.

ROW 11: Using **color D,** same as row 3.

ROW 12: Using D, same as row 4.

ROW 13: Using D, same as row 1.

ROW 14: Using D, same as row 2.

ROW 15: Using **color A,** same as row 7.

ROW 16: Using A, same as row 8.

Repeat these 16 rows.

HEADBAND:

With #3 needle and **color A,** cast on 20 stitches. Work in pattern stitch, alternating colors every 4 rows. When piece measures desired length (fits tightly around your head), bind off all stitches loosely.

FINISHING:

Sew seam. With E crochet hook and **color A,** work 2 rows of single crochet around edges.

oh brother

YARN: Filatura di Crosa, Zara (136½ yards/50g ball)

FIBER CONTENT: 100% merino wool

COLORS: MC: 1424; A: 1888; B: 1503

AMOUNT: MC: 10 (11, 12, 13); A: 1 (1, 2, 2); B: 1 (1, 2, 2) balls

TOTAL YARDAGE: MC: 1365 (1501, 1638, 1774); A: 136½ (136½, 273, 273); B: 136.5 (136½, 273, 273) yards

GAUGE: 5 stitches = 1 inch; 20 stitches = 4 inches

NEEDLE SIZE: U.S. #7 (4.5mm) for body or size needed to obtain gauge; U.S. #5 (3.75mm) for ribbing

SIZES: S (M, L, XL)

KNITTED MEASUREMENTS: Width = 22" (23½", 25", 26"); Length = 23" (24", 25", 26"); Sleeve Length = 18" (19", 19½", 20")

OTHER MATERIALS: 1 zipper

Years ago, Julie made a sweater for her younger brother, Matt. She didn't have a lot of time, so she chose a nice but chunky yarn and made him a pullover. When she gave it to him, he opened it and said, "Thanks, I like it," and, as only a brother would say, "but why didn't you make me one like the one you're wearing?" It took Julie years to get over this, and although she vowed never to knit for him again, a big birthday was coming up, so she decided to stop holding a grudge and make him the male version of the zippered cardigan she had worn. At least she knew he would like it. No smart-alec comments came out of his mouth this time, just a big thank-you.

RIBBING PATTERN:

Work all rows in K1, P1 ribbing:
Rows 1 AND 2: color A.
Rows 3 AND 4: color B.
Repeat rows 1–4 3 times.

BACK:

With #5 needle and **color A,** cast on 110 (118, 126, 130) stitches. Work in ribbing pattern. Change to #7 needle and MC and work in St st until piece measures 14" (14½", 15", 15½") from cast-on edge, ending with a WS row. SHAPE ARM-HOLES: Bind off 4 stitches at the beginning of the next 2 rows. Bind off 3 stitches at the beginning of the next 2 rows. Bind off 2 stitches at the beginning of the next 2 rows. Then decrease 1 stitch at each edge, every other row 2 (3, 4, 3) times until 88 (94, 100, 106) stitches remain. Continue to work in St st until piece measures 23" (24", 25", 26") from cast-on edge, ending with a WS row. Bind off all stitches loosely.

FRONT: (MAKE 2, REVERSE SHAPING)

With #5 needle and **color A,** cast on 56 (60, 64, 66) stitches. Work in ribbing pattern. Change to #7 needle and MC and work in St st until piece measures 14" (14½", 15", 15½") from cast-on edge, ending with a WS row for the left front and a RS row for the right front. SHAPE ARMHOLES AS FOR BACK AT SIDE EDGE ONLY until 45 (48, 51, 54) stitches remain. Continue to work in St st until piece measures 20" (21", 22", 23") from cast-on edge, ending with a RS row for the left front and a WS row for the right front. SHAPE CREW NECK: At beginning of neck edge, every other row bind off 5 stitches 1 time, 4 stitches 1 time, 3 stitches 1 time, 2 stitches 1 time, and 1 stitch 2 (2, 3, 3) times. Continue to work in St st on remaining 29 (32, 34, 37) stitches until piece measures 23" (24", 25" 26") from cast-on edge ending with a WS row. Bind off all stitches loosely.

SLEEVES:

With #5 needle and **color A,** cast on 46 (48, 50, 52) stitches. Work in ribbing pattern. Change to #7 needle and MC and work in St st. **AT THE SAME TIME,** increase 1 stitch at each edge, every 6th row 17 (18, 18, 19) times until you have 80 (84, 86, 90) stitches. *Note: Increase leaving 2 edge stitches on either side. This means you should knit 2 stitches, increase a stitch, knit to the last 2 stitches, increase a stitch, and then knit the remaining 2 stitches. Increasing like this makes it easier to sew up your seams.* When sleeve measures 18" (19", 19½", 20") from cast-on edge, ending with a WS row, SHAPE CAP: Bind off 4 stitches at the beginning of the next 2

rows. Bind off 3 stitches at the beginning of the next 2 rows. Bind off 2 stitches at the beginning of the next 2 rows. Then decrease 1 stitch at each edge, every other row 2 (3, 4, 3) times. Bind off 2 stitches at the beginning of the next 20 (20, 20, 22) rows until 18 (20, 20, 22) stitches remain. Bind off all stitches loosely.

FINISHING:

Sew shoulder seams together. Sew sleeves on. Sew up side and sleeve seams. NECK BAND: With #5 needle, **color B,** and RS facing, pick up 84 (84, 86, 86) stitches around neck. Work all rows in K1, P1 ribbing:
ROWS 1 AND 2: color B
ROWS 3 AND 4: color A

Repeat rows 1–4 3 times. Bind off all stitches loosely.
ZIPPER BANDS: With #5 needle, **color B,** and RS facing, pick up 129 (135, 141, 147) stitches up side edge. Work all rows in K1, P1 ribbing:
ROWS 1 AND 2: color B
ROWS 3 AND 4: color A

Repeat rows 1–4 3 times. Bind off all stitches loosely. Repeat on other band. Sew zipper in.

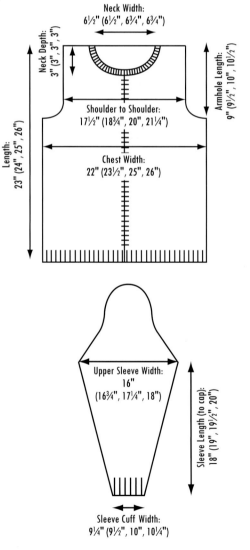

Neck Width: 6½" (6½", 6¾", 6¾")

Neck Depth: 3" (3", 3", 3")

Armhole Length: 9" (9½", 10", 10½")

Shoulder to Shoulder: 17½" (18¾", 20", 21¼")

Length: 23" (24", 25", 26")

Chest Width: 22" (23½", 25", 26")

Upper Sleeve Width: 16" (16¾", 17¼", 18")

Sleeve Length (to cap): 18" (19", 19½", 20")

Sleeve Cuff Width: 9¼" (9½", 10", 10¼")

another sweater for jeff

YARN: Rowan, Summer Tweed (118 yards/50g ball)

FIBER CONTENT: 70% silk/30% cotton

COLOR: 535

AMOUNT: 8 (9, 10, 11) balls

TOTAL YARDAGE: 944 (1062, 1180, 1298) yards

GAUGE: 4 stitches = 1 inch; 16 stitches = 4 inches

NEEDLE SIZE: U.S. #9 (5.5mm) or size needed to obtain gauge

SIZES: S (M, L, XL)

KNITTED MEASUREMENTS: Width = 21" (22½", 24", 25"); Length = 23" (24", 25", 26"); Sleeve Length = 17" (18½", 20", 21")

Jordana had made Jeff lots of sweaters over the years. Most of them were heavy, chunky sweaters—meant for the coldest winter days. Jeff, however, was not satisfied with his lot of sweaters. He wanted something for the warmer months, for those breezy nights up in the country. And although Jordana could count on one hand the number of times they were up in the country, much less on a breezy night, she agreed to make him a lighter-weight sweater. She chose a great yarn that was a silk/cotton blend; it had a slightly rugged, tweedy look; and it draped nicely. She made this basic pullover with rolled edges and an unfinished V-neck, which looked great with a pair of khaki shorts or worn-out jeans. She gave it to Jeff as a surprise on the first day of summer. Jeff loves it and, like a good, appreciative husband, wears it whenever the wind blows, even if they're not in the country.

BACK:

With #9 needle, cast on 84 (90, 96, 100) stitches. Work in St st until piece measures 14" (15", 15½", 16") from cast-on edge, ending with a WS row. SHAPE ARMHOLES: Bind off 4 stitches at the beginning of the next 2 rows. Bind off 3 stitches at the beginning of the next 2 rows. Bind off 2 stitches at the beginning of the next 2 rows. Then decrease 1 stitch at each edge 1 time until 64 (70, 76, 80) stitches remain. Continue working in St st until piece measures 23" (24", 25", 26") from cast-on edge, ending with a WS row. Bind off all stitches loosely.

FRONT:

Work as for back until piece measures 14" (15", 15½", 16") from cast-on edge, ending with a WS row. SHAPE ARM-HOLES: Bind off 4 stitches at the beginning of the next 2 rows. Bind off 3 stitches at the beginning of the next 2 rows. Bind off 2 stitches at the beginning of the next 2 rows. Then decrease 1 stitch at each edge 1 time until 64 (70, 76, 80) stitches remain. Continue working in St st until piece measures 15" (15½", 16", 16½") from cast-on edge, ending with a WS row. SHAPE V-NECK: Place a marker at the center. ROW 1: Knit until 4 stitches before the marker, K2tog, K2. Turn work around as if you were at the end of the row. Ignore the rest of the stitches. ROW 2: Purl to end of row. ROW 3: Knit. ROW 4: Purl. Repeat rows 1–4 11 (11, 12, 12) more times until 20 (23, 25, 27) stitches remain. Continue to work on these stitches until piece measures 23" (24", 25", 26") from cast-on edge, ending with a WS row. Bind off remaining stitches loosely. Attach yarn to other side. You should be on a RS row. ROW 1: K2, SSK, Knit until end. ROW 2: Purl. ROW 3: Knit. ROW 4: Purl. Repeat rows 1–4 11 (11, 12, 12) more times until 20 (23, 25, 27) stitches remain. Continue to work on these stitches until piece measures 23" (24", 25", 26") from cast-on edge, ending with a WS row. Bind off remaining stitches loosely.

SLEEVES:

With #9 needle, cast on 36 (36, 38, 40) stitches. Work in St st. **AT THE SAME TIME,** increase one stitch at each edge, every 6th row 13 (15, 16, 16) times until you have 62 (66, 70, 72) stitches. *Note: Increase leaving 2 edge stitches on either side of work. This means you should knit 2 stitches, increase a stitch, knit to the last 2 stitches, increase a stitch, and then knit the remaining 2 stitches. Increasing like this makes it easier to sew up your seams.* Continue in St st until sleeve measures 17" (18½",

20", 21") from cast-on edge, ending with a WS row. SHAPE CAP: Bind off 4 stitches at the beginning of the next 2 rows. Bind off 3 stitches at the beginning of the next 2 rows. Bind off 2 stitches at the beginning of the next 2 rows. Then decrease 1 stitch at each edge 1 time. Bind off 2 stitches at the beginning of the next 14 (16, 16, 18) rows. Bind off remaining 14 (14, 18, 16) stitches loosely.

FINISHING:

Sew shoulder seams together. Sew sleeves on and then sew down side and sleeve seams.

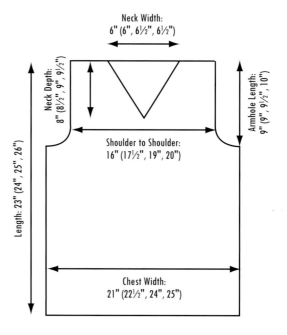

Neck Width:
6" (6", 6½", 6½")

Neck Depth:
8" (8½", 9", 9½")

Armhole Length:
9" (9", 9½", 10")

Length: 23" (24", 25", 26")

Shoulder to Shoulder:
16" (17½", 19", 20")

Chest Width:
21" (22½", 24", 25")

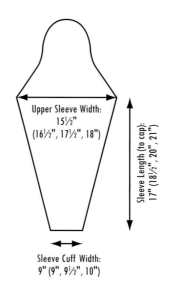

Upper Sleeve Width:
15½" (16½", 17½", 18")

Sleeve Length (to cap):
17" (18½", 20", 21")

Sleeve Cuff Width:
9" (9", 9½", 10")

summer

When people think of summer, swimming, sunbathing, or picnicking in the park are the activities that typically come to mind. Though knitting is usually not at the top of the list, we believe it should be! There are lots of great summer items to knit and tons of fabulous lightweight yarns to knit with. Tank tops, halters, skirts, shawls, and bags are just a few of the items that are fun to knit, whether you're relaxing on the beach or beating the heat in the cool of air conditioning. And natural fibers such as cotton, linen, and rayon are the perfect weight for a warm day and lend a feeling of luxury and freedom of movement.

daniele did this one

YARN: Filatura di Crosa, Malva (110 yards/50g ball)

FIBER CONTENT: 85% cotton/ 15% polyamide

COLOR: 1

AMOUNT: 4 (5, 6, 6) balls

TOTAL YARDAGE: 440 (550, 660, 660) yards

GAUGE: 4 stitches = 1 inch; 16 stitches = 4 inches

NEEDLE SIZE: U.S. #9 (5.5mm) or size needed to obtain gauge

SIZES: XS (S, M, L)

KNITTED MEASUREMENTS: Width = 16" (17", 18", 19"); Length = 21" (22", 23", 24"); Sleeve Length = 1" (1", 1½", 2")

For those of you who do not know about Daniele, she is Jordana's sister. We first introduced her as a certified "spaz knitter" who had trouble making a sweater for which both sleeves were the same length or the front lined up properly with the back. Over the years, however, Daniele has become quite a proficient knitter and has made many beautiful projects, both for herself and for various children in her life. This is one of her latest creations. It's a simple T-shirt, knit in stockinette stitch with a little ruffle around the bottoms and on the sleeves. We suggested a light-weight ribbon yarn to keep it airy. Daniele knit it up quite quickly, had no problem making the ruffles, which entailed just simple increasing and decreasing, and looked great in it. She wanted us to let everyone know how far she has come as a knitter, and that if she can do it, so can you.

BACK:

With #9 needle, cast on 128 (136, 144, 152) stitches. Work 2 rows in St st. **Next row**: Decrease by knitting 2 stitches together across the entire row—64 (68, 72, 76) stitches remain. Work 1 row of purl. Then work in St st until piece measures 14" (14½", 15", 15½") from cast-on edge, ending with a WS row.

SHAPE ARMHOLES: Bind off 3 stitches at the beginning of the next 2 rows. Bind off 2 stitches at the beginning of the next 2 rows. Then decrease 1 stitch at each edge 1 time until 52 (56, 60, 64) stitches remain. Continue working in St st until piece measures 21" (22", 23", 24") from cast-on edge, ending with a WS row. Bind off all stitches loosely.

FRONT:

Note: You will begin shaping the armhole and the V-neck at the same time. With #9 needle, cast on 128 (136, 144, 152) stitches. Work as for back until piece measures 14" (14½", 15", 15½") from cast-on edge, ending with a WS row. SHAPE ARMHOLES: Bind off 3 stitches at the beginning of the next 2

rows. Bind off 2 stitches at the beginning of the next 2 rows. Then decrease 1 stitch at each edge 1 time. **AT THE SAME TIME, SHAPE V-NECK:** Place a marker at the center. **ROW 1:** Knit until 4 stitches before the marker, K2tog, K2. Turn work around as if you were at the end of the row. Ignore the rest of the stitches. **ROW 2:** Purl to end of row. **ROW 3:** Knit to marker. **ROW 4:** Purl to end of the row. Repeat rows 1–4 5 more times until 20 (22, 24, 26) stitches remain. Then repeat rows 1 and 2 6 (7, 7, 8) times until 14 (15, 17, 18) stitches remain. Continue to work in St st on these stitches until piece measures 21" (22", 23", 24") from cast-on edge, ending with a WS row. Bind off remaining stitches loosely. Attach yarn to other side. You should be on a RS row. **ROW 1:** K2, SSK, knit until end. **ROW 2:** Purl. **ROW 3:** Knit. **ROW 4:** Purl. Repeat rows 1–4 5 more times until 20 (22, 24, 26) stitches remain. Then repeat rows 1 and 2 6 (7, 7, 8) times until 14 (15, 17, 18) stitches remain. Continue to work on these stitches until piece measures 21" (22", 23", 24") from cast-on edge, ending with a WS row. Bind off remaining stitches loosely.

SLEEVES:

With #9 needle, cast on 84 (88, 96, 104) stitches. **ROW 1:** Knit. **ROW 2:** K2tog across row. You will now have 42 (44, 48, 52) stitches. **ROW 3:** Purl. *Note: For XS and S sizes, begin to shape cap immediately. For size M, work 4 more rows in St st before shaping cap. For size L, work 6 more rows before shaping cap.* **SHAPE CAP:** Bind off 3 stitches at the beginning of the next 2 rows. Bind off 2 stitches at the beginning of the next 2 rows. Then decrease 1 stitch at each edge 1 time. Bind off 2 stitches at the beginning of the next 10 (12, 14, 14) rows until 10 (8, 8, 12) stitches remain. Bind off remaining stitches loosely.

FINISHING:

Sew shoulder seams together. Sew sleeves on and then sew down side and sleeve seams. With an H crochet hook, work 1 row single crochet around neck.

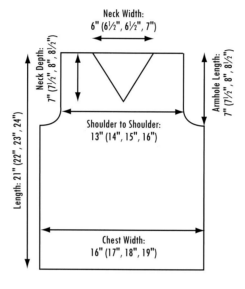

Neck Width:
6" (6½", 6½", 7")

Neck Depth:
7" (7½", 8", 8½")

Armhole Length:
7" (7½", 8", 8½")

Length: 21" (22", 23", 24")

Shoulder to Shoulder:
13" (14", 15", 16")

Chest Width:
16" (17", 18", 19")

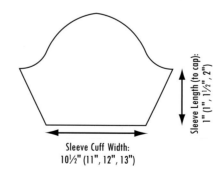

Sleeve Length (to cap):
1" (1", 1½", 2")

Sleeve Cuff Width:
10½" (11", 12", 13")

petra's blunder

YARN: A and B: Tahki, Cotton Classic (108 yards/50g ball); C: Filatura di Crosa, Pixel (176 yards/50g ball)

FIBER CONTENT: A and B: 100% cotton; C: 80% viscose/20% polyamide

COLORS: A: 3096; B: 3204; C: 10

AMOUNT: A: 3 (3, 4, 4); B: 1 (2, 2, 2); C: 3 (3, 3, 4) balls

TOTAL YARDAGE: A: 324 (324, 432, 432); B: 108 (216, 216, 216); C: 528 (528, 528, 704) yards

GAUGE: 4 stitches = 1 inch; 16 stitches = 4 inches

NEEDLE SIZE: U.S. #9 (5.5mm) or size needed to obtain gauge; I (5mm) crochet hook

SIZES: XS (S, M, L)

KNITTED MEASUREMENTS: Width = 15" (16", 17", 18"); Length = 21" (22", 23", 24")

*Yarn is worked double throughout the sweater—this means you should hold 1 strand of **A** or **B** together with 1 strand of **C** as if they were 1.*

*When piece measures 13" (14", 15", 16") from cast-on edge, you will hold 3 strands of **color C** together as if they were one and work in St st for 1".*

One day at The Yarn Company, Petra and Julie wanted to knit up a sample tank top—one that was quick and simple but at the same time unique. They found a beautiful multicolored yarn they liked, but it was very thin and would not be a quick knit. Julie and Petra decided to try doubling this yarn with a solid yarn. It looked great, but something wasn't quite perfect. After bouncing numerous ideas around, they finally decided to use two different solid colors separated by a stripe of the multicolored yarn in the middle. This added just the right bit of uniqueness. Then, as Petra was knitting the tank top, she spaced out and forgot to finish the neck shaping. When she completed the first side of the neck, she looked at it and laughed at her mistake. But she liked the way it came out. The result was a square neck, and we loved it.

BACK:

With #9 needle and 1 strand of **color A** and 1 strand of **color C,** cast on 60 (64, 68, 72) stitches. Work in St st until piece measures 13" (14", 15", 16") from cast-on edge, ending with a WS row. Cut **color A** and work with 3 strands of **color C** for 1". Cut 2 strands of **color C** and work with 1 strand of **color B** and 1 strand of **color C.** Continue to work in St st. **AT THE SAME TIME,** when piece measures 14½" (15", 15½", 16") from cast-on edge, ending with a WS row, **SHAPE ARMHOLES:** Bind off 3 stitches at the beginning of the next 2 rows. Bind off 2 stitches at the beginning of the next 2 rows. Then decrease 1 stitch at each edge, every other row 3 times until 44 (48, 52, 56) stitches remain. Continue working in St st until piece measures 21" (22", 23", 24") from cast-on edge, ending with a WS row. Bind off all stitches loosely.

FRONT:

With #9 needle, 1 strand of **color A** and 1 strand of **color C,** cast on 60 (64, 68, 72) stitches. Work as for back, changing colors where noted until piece measures 14½" (15", 15½", 16") from cast-on edge, ending with a WS row. **SHAPE ARMHOLES:** Bind off 3 stitches at the beginning of the next 2 rows. Bind off 2 stitches at the beginning of the next 2 rows. Then decrease 1 stitch at

each edge, every other row 3 times until 44 (48, 52, 56) stitches remain. Continue working in St st until piece measures 16" (17", 18", 19") from cast-on edge, ending with a WS row. **SHAPE NECK:** Bind off center 20 (22, 24, 26) stitches. With no further decreasing, continue working each side separately until piece measures 21" (22", 23", 24") from cast-on edge, ending with a WS row. Bind off all stitches loosely.

FINISHING:

Sew shoulder seams together. Sew side seams. With an I crochet hook and 2 strands of **color A,** work 1 row single crochet around neckline and armholes. Then, with 2 strands of **color B,** work 1 row of single crochet around the bottom edge of the tank.

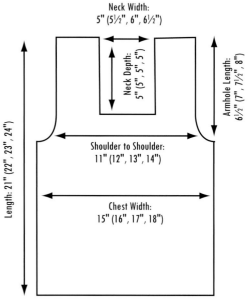

Neck Width:
5" (5½", 6", 6½")

Neck Depth:
5" (5", 5", 5")

Armhole Length:
6½" (7", 7½", 8")

Shoulder to Shoulder:
11" (12", 13", 14")

Length: 21" (22", 23", 24")

Chest Width:
15" (16", 17", 18")

flirty skirt

YARN: GGH, Domino (136½ yards/50g ball)

FIBER CONTENT: 44% cotton/43% acrylic/13% polyester

COLOR: 177-004

AMOUNT: 5 (6, 7, 8) balls

TOTAL YARDAGE: 683 (819, 955, 1092) yards

GAUGE: 5½ stitches = 1 inch; 22 stitches = 4 inches

NEEDLE SIZE: For seamed version: U.S. #5 (3.75mm) or size needed to obtain gauge; U.S. #3 (2.5mm) for ribbing; 24" circular U.S. #5 (3¾mm) for frill

For circular version: 24" circular U.S. #5 (3.75mm) or size needed to obtain gauge; circular 24" U.S. #3 (2.5mm) for ribbing; 24" circular U.S. #5 for frill

SIZES: XS (S, M, L)

One hot, sticky summer afternoon, Laura floated into our store looking like a breath of fresh air. She was wearing an adorable skirt with a ruffle on the bottom, a cute tank, and a snazzy pair of flip-flops. Unlike so many of the customers who'd come in that day looking sweaty and tired, Laura looked cool, comfortable, and at ease. She wanted to make a skirt like the one she was wearing. And although we hadn't written skirt patterns that often, we jumped at the chance to duplicate her cute skirt. We found the perfect yarn, which had a slight nubby texture, came in great summery colors, and had a light feel when worn. We then wrote the pattern, which was just a simple tube, more or less, put a ruffle on the bottom, and suggested an I-cord drawstring for the top to hold it up, just in case.

SEAMED VERSION
SKIRT: (MAKE 2)

With #5 needle, cast on 90 (92, 96, 100) stitches. Work in St st until piece measures 11½" (12", 13", 14½") from cast-on edge, ending with a WS row. Then decrease 1 stitch at each end of every 4th row 5 times until 80 (82, 86, 90) stitches remain. *Decrease as follows: K2, K2tog, knit to last 4 stitches, SSK, K2.* Change to #3 needle and work in K1, P1 ribbing for 1½". **AT THE SAME**

TIME, decrease 1 stitch at each end of every other row 3 times until 74 (76, 80, 84) stitches remain. When the ribbing measures ³/₄", make loopholes as follows: K3 (4, 3, 5) *K2tog, YO, K4* repeat from * to *, end K2tog, YO, K3 (4, 3, 5). Continue in K1, P1 ribbing for another ³/₄", then bind off all stitches loosely.

FRILL:

With #5 circular needle and RS facing, pick up 90 (92, 96, 100) stitches across bottom of skirt. Purl 1 row. Then,

increase across the row by knitting into the front and back of each stitch. You will now have 180 (184, 192, 200) stitches. Continue working in St st for 1½". Work 4 rows in garter stitch. Bind off all stitches loosely.

I-CORD:

With #3 needle, make a 3-stitch I-cord.

FINISHING:

Sew seams of skirt together. Thread I-cord through holes.

CIRCULAR VERSION
SKIRT:

With #5 circular needle, cast on 180 (184, 192, 200) stitches. Work in St st for 11½" (12", 13", 14½") from cast-on edge. *Note: After your cast-on row, knit 90 (92, 96, 100) stitches, place marker, knit 90 (92, 96, 100) stitches, place marker. You will now have two markers dividing front and back.* Then decrease 4 stitches, every 4th round 5 times as follows: slip marker, K1, K2tog, work to 3 stitches before 2nd marker, SSK, K1, slip marker, K1, K2tog, work to 3 stitches before 1st marker, SSK, K1. Change to #3 needle and work K1, P1 ribbing for 1½". **AT THE SAME TIME,** decrease 4 stitches, every other round 3 times until 148 (152, 160, 168) stitches remain. When the ribbing measures ¾", work 1 row of loopholes as follows: K4 (3, 1, 2) *K2tog, YO, K4* repeat from * to *, end K2tog, YO, K4 (3, 1, 2). Continue in K1, P1 ribbing for another ¾", then bind off all stitches loosely.

FRILL:

With #5 circular needle and RS facing, pick up 180 (184, 192, 200) stitches across bottom of skirt. Knit 1 row. Then, increase across the round by knitting into the front and back of each stitch. You will now have 360 (368, 384, 400) stitches. Continue working in St st for 1½". Work 4 rows in garter stitch. Bind off all stitches loosely.

I-CORD:

With #3 needle, make a 3-stitch I-cord.

FINISHING:

Thread I-cord through holes.

Skirt Width:
16¼" (16¾", 17½", 18")

Skirt Length (to frill):
16" (16½", 17½", 19")

sexy mama

YARN: GGH, Mystik (115 yards/50g ball)

FIBER CONTENT: 54% cotton/46% viscose

COLOR: 68

AMOUNT: 5 (5, 6, 7) balls

TOTAL YARDAGE: 575 (575, 690, 805) yards

GAUGE: 5 stitches = 1 inch; 20 stitches = 4 inches (in cable pattern)

NEEDLE SIZE: U.S. #9 (5.5 mm) for body or size needed to obtain gauge; 24" circular U.S. #7 (4.5mm) for ribbing; I (5.5mm) crochet hook

SIZES: XS (S, M, L)

KNITTED MEASUREMENTS: Width = 14½" (15¼", 16", 17¾"); Length = 18" (18½", 19½", 20¼")

Yarn is worked double throughout the halter—this means you should hold 2 strands of yarn together as if they were 1.

Jenny had given birth to a beautiful baby girl in March. And, just like all the stars that you read about, she was back to her pre-baby body within weeks—which was quite a good body, by the way. Despite the fact that everyone was "oohing" and "aahing" over her quick weight loss and her adorable baby, Jenny said that she felt "blah" and wanted to knit something that would make her feel sexy. We designed this cute cabled halter top for her to show off her strong shoulders, toned back, and amazingly flat abs. We used some increasing for the darts up front to add subtle shape. She finished it quickly and—when she wore it in with her three-month-old in tow—she truly was a sexy mama.

PATTERN STITCH:

C6B (cable 6 into back): Place 3 stitches on a cable needle, hold at back of the work, K3 from left-hand needle, K3 from cable needle.

FRONT:

With #7 needle and 2 strands of yarn, cast on 58 (62, 66, 70) stitches. Work in K1, P1 ribbing for 1". Change to #9 needle and work in pattern as follows:

ROW 1: K13 (14, 15, 16), P2, K6, P2, K12 (14, 16, 18), P2, K6, P2, K13 (14, 15, 16).

ROW 2: P13 (14, 15, 16), K2, P6, K2, P12 (14, 16, 18), K2, P6, K2, P13 (14, 15, 16).

ROW 3: K13 (14, 15, 16), P2, C6B, P2, K12 (14, 16, 18), P2, C6B, P2, K13 (14, 15, 16).

ROW 4: Same as row 2.

ROW 5: Same as row 1.

ROW 6: Same as row 1.

AT THE SAME TIME, on the 7th and every 6th row thereafter, increase 1 stitch 5 stitches before the first purl and 5 stitches after the last purl, until you have 72 (76, 80, 84) stitches. For example, on row 7: K8 (9, 10, 11), inc 1, K5, P2, K6, P2, K12 (14, 16, 18), P2, K6, P2, K5, inc 1, K8 (9, 10, 11). When piece measures 11" (12", 13", 14") from cast-on edge, ending with a WS row, SHAPE ARMHOLES: Decrease 1 stitch at each end of every row (K2tog on the knit rows and P2tog on the purl rows) 26 (28, 30, 32) times until 20 stitches remain. Change to #7 needle and work in K1, P1 ribbing for 1". Bind off all stitches loosely.

BACK:

With #7 needle and 2 strands of yarn, cast on 36 (40, 44, 48) stitches. Work in K1, P1 ribbing for 1". Change to #9 needle and work in St st until piece measures 11" (12", 13", 14") from cast-on edge, ending with a WS row. Bind off all stitches loosely.

FINISHING:

Sew sides together. With #7 circular needle and RS facing you, beginning at the top of the right front, pick up stitches down right front, stitches across back, and stitches up left front. Work in K1, P1 ribbing for 1". Bind off all stitches loosely.

With an I crochet hook, make 2 chains (approximately 12"–14"). Attach each chain to top front of the halter.

Neck Width:
7½" (8", 8½", 9")

Armhole Length:
7" (6½", 6½", 6¼")

Length: 18" (18½", 19½", 20¼")

Chest Width:
14½" (15¼", 16", 16¾")

the suggestive shrug

YARN: Louet Sales, Euroflax (270 yards/100g ball)

FIBER CONTENT: 100% linen

COLOR: Emerald

AMOUNT: 3 (3, 3, 4) balls

TOTAL YARDAGE: 810 (810, 810, 1080) yards

STITCH GAUGE: 3¾ stitches = 1 inch; 15 stitches = 4 inches

ROW GAUGE: 5 rows = 1 inch; 20 rows = 4 inches

NEEDLE SIZE: U.S. #10 (6mm) or size needed to obtain gauge; E (3.5mm) crochet hook

SIZES: XS (S, M, L)

KNITTED MEASUREMENTS: Width = 16" (17", 18½", 20"); Length = 16" (17", 18½", 20"); Sleeve Length = 16½" (17", 17½", 18")

When Wendy comes into our store, she gets sensory overload. Her eyes dart from one sample to the next, and you can almost see her salivating and plotting her next purchase. One bright summer's day, Wendy walked in and was determined not to look at anything. She kept her head down, sat at the table, and began to work diligently at finishing up one of her many projects. The air conditioning, however, was giving her a slight chill—so we offered her this shrug to put on over her tank top. She put it on, sat quietly for a few minutes, and then began looking at herself. She let out a short and sudden scream and said, "Now I have to knit one!! I wasn't going to buy any yarn today . . . but now I have to!" While our intent had merely been to warm her up, the shrug did look great on her, so we didn't argue. We helped her pick out the perfect color of linen yarn—which will only become softer and drapier with each wash and dry. And then we watched her walk out with yet another Yarn Company shopping bag.

BACK:

With #10 needle, cast on 60 (64, 70, 76) stitches. Work in St st until piece measures 8½" (9", 10", 11") from cast-on edge, ending with a WS row. SHAPE ARMHOLES: At beginning of the next 2 rows bind off 3 stitches. Then decrease 1 stitch at each edge, every other row 2 (3, 5, 7) times until 50 (52, 54, 56) stitches remain. Continue to work in St st until piece measures 16" (17", 18½", 20") from cast-on edge, ending with a WS row. Bind off all stitches loosely.

FRONT: (MAKE 2, REVERSE SHAPING)

Note: You will begin shaping the neck at 2". At 8½" (9", 10", 11") you will begin shaping armhole.

With #10 needle, cast on 56 (60, 66, 70) stitches. Work in St st until piece measures 2", ending with a WS row. SHAPE V-NECK: Left front: ROW 1: Knit until 4 stitches remain, K2tog, K2. ROW 2: Purl. Work rows 1 and 2 35 (36, 37, 38) times more. Right front: ROW 1: K2, SSK, knit to end. ROW 2: Purl. Work rows 1 and 2 35 (36, 37, 38) times more. **AT THE SAME TIME,** when work measures 8½" (9", 10", 11") from the cast-on edge, ending with a WS row for the left front and a RS row for the right front, SHAPE ARMHOLES AS FOR BACK AT OUTSIDE EDGE ONLY. Continue to work in St st, decreasing at the neck edge, until 15 (17, 20, 21) stitches remain and piece measures 16" (17", 18½", 20") from cast-on edge, ending with a WS row. Bind off all stitches loosely.

SLEEVES:

With #10 needle, cast on 30 (32, 34, 36) stitches. Then work in St st. **AT THE SAME TIME,** increase 1 stitch at each edge, every 10th (10th, 8th, 8th) row 7 (8, 9, 10) times until you have 44 (48, 52, 56) stitches. *Note: Increase leaving 2 edge stitches on either side. This means you should knit 2 stitches, increase a stitch, knit to the last 2 stitches, increase a stitch, and then knit the remaining 2 stitches. Increasing like this makes it easier to sew up your seams.* When sleeve measures 16½" (17", 17½", 18") from cast-on edge, ending with a WS row, SHAPE CAP: Bind off 3 stitches at the beginning of the next 2 rows. Then decrease 1 stitch at each edge, every other row 2 (3, 5, 7) times. Bind off 2 stitches at the beginning of the next 12 rows until 10 (12, 12, 12) stitches remain. Bind off all stitches loosely.

FINISHING:

Sew shoulder seams together. Sew sleeves on. Sew side and sleeve seams. With an E crochet hook, work 1 row of single crochet around all edges.

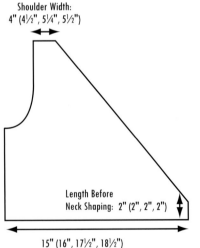

Shoulder Width:
4" (4½", 5¼", 5½")

Length Before
Neck Shaping: 2" (2", 2", 2")

15" (16", 17½", 18½")

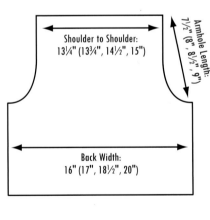

Shoulder to Shoulder:
13¼" (13¾", 14½", 15")

Armhole Length:
7½" (8", 8½", 9")

Back Width:
16" (17", 18½", 20")

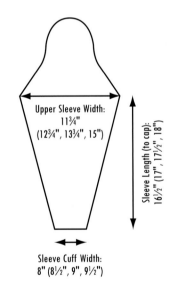

Upper Sleeve Width:
11¾"
(12¾", 13¾", 15")

Sleeve Length (to cap):
16½" (17", 17½", 18")

Sleeve Cuff Width:
8" (8½", 9", 9½")

suzanne's bright idea

YARN: Tahki, Dream (272 yards/50g ball)

FIBER CONTENT: 80% wool/20% nylon

COLORS: A: 25; B: 28

AMOUNT: A: 9 (10, 11, 12) B:
2 (2, 2, 2) balls

TOTAL YARDAGE: A: 2448 (2720, 2992,
3264); B: 544 yards

GAUGE: 5¾ stitches = 1 inch; 23 stitches
= 4 inches

NEEDLE SIZE: U.S. #7 (4.5mm) or size
needed to obtain gauge; U.S. #5
(3.75mm) for trim; G (4mm) crochet hook

SIZES: XS (S, M, L)

KNITTED MEASUREMENTS: Bottom
Width = 22½" (24", 25¼", 26½");
Chest Width = 16" (17", 18", 19"); Length
= 33" (35", 37", 39")

*Yarn is worked double throughout the
dress—this means you should hold
2 strands of yarn together as if they
were 1.*

In mid-January, on a cold, cold day, Suzanne, our manager, and Jordana were fantasizing about knitting and wearing tanks, skirts, and dresses. Then, UPS came and delivered Dream, a yarn that would be perfect, if knit doubled, for a dress. We agreed on a color and put it away until we were ready to knit it. In late February, Suzanne walked into work one morning and announced, "Hey, guys, I have a great idea. We should really knit a dress out of Dream doubled!" We looked at each other, laughed, and said, "That's a great idea, Suzanne!" Can you say Déjà vu?

BACK:

With #5 needle and 2 strands of **color B,** cast on 130 (138, 146, 152) stitches. Work in St st for 1½" (1½", 2", 2"). Work 1 purl row on the RS. Continue in St st for 1½" (1½", 2", 2") more. Change to # 7 needle and 2 strands of **color A.** Work in St st and, **AT THE SAME TIME,** decrease 1 stitch at each edge, every 6th row 19 (20, 21, 21) times until 92 (98, 104, 110) stitches remain. Continue in St st with no further decreasing until piece measures 26" (27½", 29", 30½") from cast-on edge, ending with a WS row. SHAPE ARMHOLES: Bind off 3 stitches at the beginning of the next 2

rows. Bind off 2 stitches at the beginning of the next 2 rows. Then decrease 1 stitch at each edge, every other row 6 (7, 7, 7) times until 70 (74, 80, 86) stitches remain. Continue working in St st until piece measures 33" (35", 37", 39") from cast-on edge, ending with a WS row. Bind off all stitches loosely.

FRONT:

Work as for back until piece measures 26" (27½", 29", 30½") from cast-on edge. SHAPE ARMHOLES: Bind off 3 stitches at the beginning of the next 2 rows. Bind off 2 stitches at the beginning of the next 2 rows. Then, decrease 1 stitch at each edge, every

other row 6 (7, 7, 7) times until 70 (74, 80, 86) stitches remain. Continue working in St st until piece measures 30" (32", 34", 36") from cast-on edge, ending with a WS row. SHAPE CREW NECK: Bind off center 20 stitches. Then, begin working each side of the neck separately. At the beginning of each neck edge, every other row bind off 4 stitches 1 time, 3 stitches 1 time, 2 stitches 1 time, and 1 stitch 1 (2, 3, 4) time(s). Continue to work on remaining 15 (16, 18, 20) stitches with no further decreasing until piece measures 33" (35", 37", 39") from cast-on edge, ending with a WS row. Bind off all stitches loosely.

FINISHING:

Sew shoulder seams together. Sew side seams. At bottom of dress, fold B color hem at purl ridge. Sew it down at inside of dress. With a G crochet hook and 2 strands of **color B,** work 3 rows of single crochet around neck and armholes.

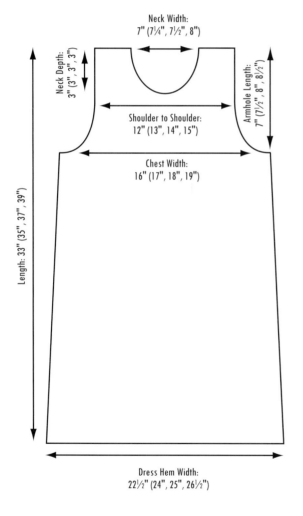

Neck Width:
7" (7¼", 7½", 8")

Neck Depth:
3" (3", 3", 3")

Armhole Length:
7" (7½", 8", 8½")

Shoulder to Shoulder:
12" (13", 14", 15")

Chest Width:
16" (17", 18", 19")

Length: 33" (35", 37", 39")

Dress Hem Width:
22½" (24", 25", 26½")

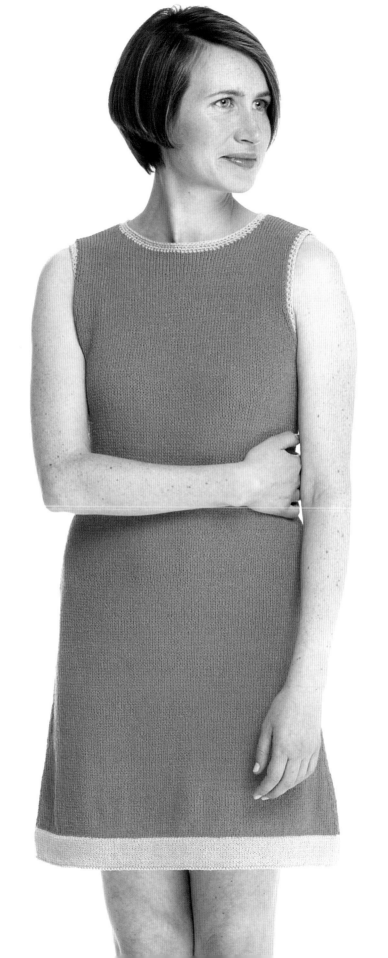

adding a little zing

YARN: S. Charles, Victoria (72 yards/50g ball)

FIBER CONTENT: 60% cotton/40% viscose

COLOR: 100

AMOUNT: 6 balls

TOTAL YARDAGE: 432 yards

GAUGE: 2½ stitches = 1 inch; 10 stitches = 4 inches in pattern

NEEDLE SIZE: U.S. #17 (12mm) or size needed to obtain gauge

SIZES: One size

KNITTED MEASUREMENTS: Width = 16"; Length = 70"

Allison was going to a July wedding on Nantucket. It was a formal affair, so she'd picked out a cute dress to wear that would be appropriate. But the dress, by itself, was a little boring. She needed an accessory that would add a little pizzazz to her outfit. So Allison came in and told us she wanted to make a shawl that would knit up quickly (the wedding was two weeks away) and liven up her outfit. We picked out this pretty open stitch and a beautiful yarn in a vibrant color. Allison wove her ends in on the ferry and wore the airy shawl to the wedding. She reported back to us that the shawl definitely did the trick and added just the right amount of "zing" to her outfit.

PATTERN STITCH (WORKED OVER EVEN NUMBER OF STITCHES):

ROW 1: K1, *YO, K2tog; repeat from *, end K1.
ROW 2: Purl.
ROW 3: K2, *YO, K2tog; repeat from *, end K2.
ROW 4: Purl.
Repeat rows 1–4 to form pattern.

SHAWL:

With #17 needle, cast on 42 stitches. Work in pattern stitch until piece measures 70". Bind off all stitches loosely.

the beach tote

YARN: Tahki, Cotton Classic (108 yards/50g ball)

FIBER CONTENT: 100% cotton

COLORS: MC: 3814; CC: 3353

AMOUNT: MC: 6; CC 3 balls

TOTAL YARDAGE: MC: 648; CC: 324 yards

GAUGE: 4½ stitches = 1 inch; 18 stitches = 4 inches

NEEDLE SIZE: U.S. #8 (5mm) or size needed to obtain gauge; U.S. # 7 (4.5mm); U.S. #6 (4mm); U.S. #5 (3.75mm); G (4mm) crochet hook

SIZES: One size

KNITTED MEASUREMENTS: Width = 14"; Length = 9½"; Depth = 7½"

Yarn is worked double throughout the bag—this means you should hold 2 strands of yarn together as if they were 1.

Yvonne was moving to sunny Los Angeles to live on the beach. Her four best friends (and knitting buddies) wanted to send her off with gifts all relating to the beach. They bought beach towels, beach balls, beach umbrellas—you get the idea. Since they all knit, they wanted a knitting project they could all work on. But they did not want to knit a garment because they were worried about gauge. So they thought of knitting a beach bag. We designed this beach tote, and they all took turns knitting it. Yvonne uses it all the time.

BASE:

With #7 needle and 2 strands of **CC**, cast on 36 stitches. Work in St st for 14". Bind off all stitches loosely.

BAG:

With #8 needle, 2 strands of **MC, and WS facing, begin at the midpoint of a short side of the base and pick up 17 stitches to corner, place marker (pm), pick up 1 stitch in the corner, pm, pick up 57 stitches to next corner, pm, pick up 1 stitch in corner, pm, pick up 17 stitches to midpoint of other short side. Knit one row, then beginning with a knit row, work in St st as follows:

ROW 1 (RS): K17, slip 1 purlwise, K57, slip 1 purlwise, K17.

ROW 2 (WS): Purl.

Repeat rows 1 and 2 until piece measures 8" ending with a WS row. Then work as follows:

ROW 1: K17, slip 1 purlwise, K14, SSK, K25, K2tog, K14, slip 1 purlwise, K17.

ROW 2: Purl.

ROW 3: K17, slip 1 purlwise, K14, SSK, K23, K2tog, K14, slip 1 purlwise, K17.

ROW 4: Purl.

ROW 5: K17, slip 1 purlwise, K14, SSK, K21, K2tog, K14, slip 1 purlwise, K17.

ROW 6: Purl.

Change to #6 needle. Work as follows:

ROW 1: K17, slip 1 purlwise, K51, slip 1 purlwise, K17.

ROW 2: Purl.

ROW 3: K8, YO, K2tog, K7, slip 1 purlwise, K51, slip 1 purlwise, K7, K2tog, YO, K8.

ROW 4: Purl.

ROW 5: K17, slip 1 purlwise, K51, slip 1 purlwise, K17.

ROW 6: Purl.

ROW 7: K17, slip 1 purlwise, K51, slip 1 purlwise, K17.

Change to #5 needle. Knit 1 row.

Change to **CC** and work as follows:

ROW 1: K17, slip 1 purlwise, K14, slip next 4 sts to holder, K27, slip next 4 sts to holder, K10, slip 1 purlwise, k17.

ROW 2: Purl, casting on 4 stitches where the holders are.

ROW 3: K17, slip 1 purlwise, K51, slip 1 purlwise, K17.

ROW 4: Purl.

ROW 5: K17, slip 1 purlwise, K51, slip 1 purlwise, K17.

ROW 6: Purl.

ROW 7: K8, YO, K2tog, K7, slip 1 purlwise, K51, slip 1 purlwise, K7, K2tog, YO, K8.

ROW 8: K17, slip 1 purlwise, K51, slip 1 purlwise, K17.

ROW 9: Purl.

Bind off all stitches loosely.

Repeat from ** picking up stitches along other half of bag.

FINISHING:

STRAPS:

With RS of bag facing, #5 needle, and **MC,** knit across 4 stitches from holder. Purl 1 row. On next row, increase 1 stitch at each edge (6 stitches). Work in St st until piece measures 14". On last row, decrease 1 stitch at each edge (4 stitches). Place these stitches on a holder.

With WS of bag facing, # 5 needle, and **CC,** pick up 4 stitches where 4 cast on stitches are. Purl 1 row. Increase 1 stitch at each edge (6 stitches). Work in St st until piece measures 14". On last row, decrease 1 stitch at each edge (4 stitches). Bind off these stitches.

Sew up side seams of bag.

Sew up seams of handles.

Sew 2 loose ends of handles to the back. For the MC, use the 2 needle bind-off method. For the CC, use normal sewing techniques.

I-CORDS: (MAKE 2)

With #5 needle and 2 strands of **CC,** cast on 3 stitches. Make a 22" I-cord. Insert I-cords into holes on gusset.

BUTTON LOOP:

With **MC** and G crochet hook, work 22 chain stitches in the center of the top and attach where you began to make a button loop. Sew a button in center of handles on the other side.

Cut out a piece of thick cardboard to fit inside the bottom of bag and place it securely inside.

don't mess with a good thing

YARN: Blue Sky Alpacas, Blue Sky Cotton (150 yards/100g ball)

FIBER CONTENT: 100% cotton

COLORS: A: 614; B: 623

AMOUNT: A: 5 (5, 6, 6); B: 3 (3, 4, 4) balls

TOTAL YARDAGE: A: 750 (750, 900, 900); B: 450 (450, 600, 600) yards

STITCH GAUGE: 4 stitches = 1 inch; 16 stitches = 4 inches

ROW GAUGE: 6 rows = 1 inch; 24 rows = 4 inches

NEEDLE SIZE: U.S. #9 (5.5 mm) or size needed to obtain gauge

SIZES: S (M, L, XL)

KNITTED MEASUREMENTS: Width = 22" (23½", 25", 26"); Length = 23" (24", 25", 26"); Sleeve Length = 18" (19", 19½", 20")

We really have Kevin to thank for this sweater design. One thing about Kevin is that he knew a good thing when he saw it. He was a very good knitter and would knit various gifts for others, but he would always make the same sweater in the same gauge for himself. They never looked the same because he would use different yarns and colors, but he would always find a yarn that got four stitches and six rows per inch. We told him that we could help him change his pattern so that he could use either a chunkier yarn or a thinner one—but he never wanted to. His sweaters always came out great, and they looked perfect on him, so he did not want to mess with a good thing. We liked them, too: we added in our own striped twist, made different sizes, and tweaked a few things, but this is Kevin's everyday sweater—a classic raglan knit in a soft, light cotton.

STRIPE PATTERN:

4 rows St st in **color A.**
2 rows St st in **color B.**

BACK AND FRONT:

With #9 needle, cast on 88 (94, 100, 104) stitches. Work in St st stripe pattern stitch until piece measures 13½" (13½", 14", 14½") from cast-on edge, ending with a WS row. **SHAPE RAGLAN ARMHOLES:** Bind off 2 stitches at the beginning of the next 2 rows. Then work **ROW 1:** K2, SSK, knit to end. **ROW 2:** P2, P2tog, purl to end.

Repeat rows 1 and 2 27 (29, 31, 33) more times until 28 (30, 32, 32) stitches remain. Bind off all stitches loosely.

SLEEVES:

With #9 needle, cast on 36 (38, 40, 40) stitches. Work in St st stripe pattern. **AT THE SAME TIME,** increase 1 stitch at each edge, every 6th row 15 (16, 16, 18) times until 66 (70, 72, 76) stitches remain. *Note: Increase leaving 2 edge stitches on either side of work. This means you should knit 2 stitches, increase a stitch, knit to the last 2 stitches, increase a stitch, and then knit the remaining 2 stitches. Increasing like this makes it easier to sew up your seams.* Continue in St st until sleeve measures 18" (19", 19½", 20") from cast-on edge, ending with a WS row. S H A P E R A G L A N S L E E V E : Bind off 2 stitches at the beginning of the next 2 rows. Then work ROW 1: K2, SSK, knit to end. ROW 2: P2, P2tog, purl to end. ROW 3: Knit. ROW 4: Purl. Repeat rows 1–4 1 (1, 2, 2) more time(s). Then repeat rows 1 and 2 24 (26, 26, 28) until 10 stitches remain. Bind off all stitches loosely.

FINISHING:

Sew raglan pieces together.

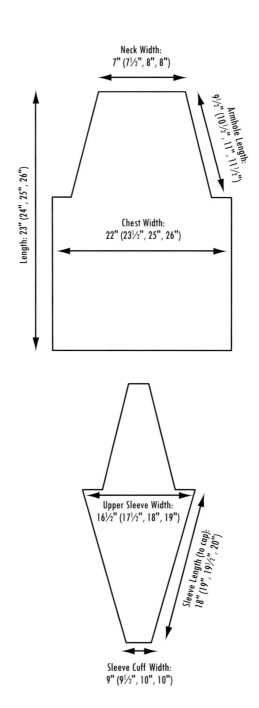

Neck Width:
7" (7½", 8", 8")

Armhole Length:
9½" (10½", 11", 11½")

Length: 23" (24", 25", 26")

Chest Width:
22" (23½", 25", 26")

Upper Sleeve Width:
16½" (17½", 18", 19")

Sleeve Length (to cap):
18" (19", 19½", 20")

Sleeve Cuff Width:
9" (9½", 10", 10")

the beach sweater

YARN: Louet Sales, Euroflax (270 yards/ 100g ball)

FIBER CONTENT: 100% linen

COLOR: 43

AMOUNT: 6 (7, 8, 9) balls

TOTAL YARDAGE: 1620 (1890, 2160, 2430) yards

GAUGE: 3¼ stitches = 1 inch; 13 stitches = 4 inches

NEEDLE SIZE: U.S. #10 (6mm) or size needed to obtain gauge

SIZES: S (M, L, XL)

KNITTED MEASUREMENTS: Width = 21" (22½", 24", 25"); Length = 23" (24", 25", 26"); Sleeve Length = 17" (18½", 20", 21")

Yarn is worked double throughout the sweater—this means you should hold 2 strands of yarn together as if they were 1.

Andrew spends summers at the beach. It's a big social scene out there, and it's ever so important to be well dressed. Andrew felt that his wardrobe was up to the strict standards of the beach crowd, but he also felt he was missing the perfect sweater for cool nights when he might be taking a romantic stroll by the ocean. This linen sweater, knit in a slightly open garter stitch, was exactly what Andrew was looking for. It had the perfect drape, looked worn but not ragged, and blended in perfectly with his wardrobe. He bribed us to make it for him by offering us a week out at his beach house. Who could resist?

BACK:

With #10 needle and 2 strands of yarn, cast on 68 (74, 78, 82) stitches. Work in garter stitch until piece measures 14" (15", 15½", 16") from cast-on edge. SHAPE ARMHOLES: Bind off 3 stitches at the beginning of the next 2 rows. Bind off 2 stitches at the beginning of the following 2 rows. Bind off 1 stitch at the beginning of the following 6 (8, 8, 8) rows until 52 (56, 60, 64) stitches remain. Continue working in garter stitch until piece measures 23" (24", 25", 26") from cast-on edge, ending with a WS row. Bind off all stitches loosely.

FRONT:

Work as for back until piece measures 14" (15", 15½", 16") from cast-on edge, ending with a WS row. SHAPE ARMHOLES: Bind off 3 stitches at the beginning of the next 2 rows. Bind off 2 stitches at the beginning of the following 2 rows. Bind off 1 stitch at the beginning of the following 6 (8, 8, 8) rows until 52 (56, 60, 64) stitches remain. Continue working in garter stitch until piece measures 16½" (17", 18", 18½") from cast-on edge. SHAPE V-NECK: Place a marker at the center. ROW 1: Knit until 4 stitches before the marker, K2tog, K2. Turn work around as if you were at the end of the row. Ignore the rest of the stitches. ROW 2: Knit. Repeat rows 1 and 2 9 (9, 10, 11) more times until 17 (19, 20, 21) stitches remain. Continue to work on these stitches until piece measures 23" (24", 25", 26") from cast-on edge, ending with a WS row. Bind off remaining stitches loosely. Attach yarn to other side. You should be on a RS row. ROW 1: K2, SSK, knit until end. ROW 2: Knit. Repeat rows 1 and 2 9 (9, 10, 11) more times until 17 (19, 20, 21) stitches remain. Continue to work on these stitches until piece measures 23" (24", 25", 26") from cast-on edge, ending with a WS row. Bind off remaining stitches loosely.

SLEEVES:

With #10 needle and 2 strands of yarn, cast on 28 (30, 32, 32) stitches. Work in garter stitch. **AT THE SAME TIME,** increase 1 stitch at each edge, every 8th row 10 (11, 12, 13) times until you have 48 (52, 56, 58) stitches. *Note: Increase leaving 2 edge stitches on either side. This means you should knit 2 stitches, increase a stitch, knit to the last 2 stitches, increase a stitch, and then knit the remaining 2 stitches. Increasing like this makes it easier to sew up your seams.* When sleeve measures 17" (18½", 20", 21") from cast-on edge, ending with a WS row, S H A P E C A P : Bind off 3 stitches at the beginning of the next 2 rows. Bind off 2 stitches at the beginning of the next 2 rows. Then bind off 1 stitch at the beginning of the following 6 (8, 8, 8) rows. Bind off 2 stitches at the beginning of the next 10 (12, 14, 14) rows until 12 (10, 10, 12) stitches remain. Bind off all stitches loosely.

FINISHING:

Sew shoulder seams together. Sew sleeves on. Then sew up side and sleeve seams.

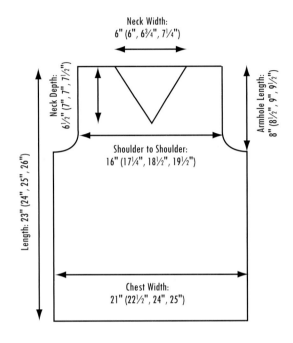

Neck Width:
6" (6", 6¾", 7¼")

Neck Depth:
6½" (7", 7", 7½")

Armhole Length:
8" (8½", 9", 9½")

Shoulder to Shoulder:
16" (17¼", 18½", 19½")

Length: 23" (24", 25", 26")

Chest Width:
21" (22½", 24", 25")

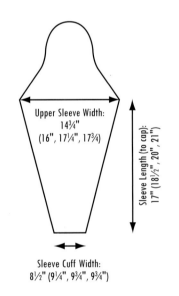

Upper Sleeve Width:
14¾"
(16", 17¼", 17¾)

Sleeve Length (to cap):
17" (18½", 20", 21")

Sleeve Cuff Width:
8½" (9¼", 9¾", 9¾")

fall

Fall is a time of endless possibilities for the knitter. As the days get cooler and the nights crisper, we knitters are dreaming of soft wools, luxurious alpacas, and evenings spent curled up with a set of needles in hand. We are excited to trade in our favorite tanks and skirts so that sweaters can find their way back into our wardrobes. We look forward to preparing for the long winter season ahead by knitting sweaters to keep us warm and gifts to give during the holidays. The projects in this chapter are inspired by the changing colors of the leaves. We've chosen crimson, fiery red, maroon, ruddy orange, deep yellows, and eggplant to reflect the colors of the season. The fibers consist primarily of alpaca and merino wool, which are warm but come in a range of weights to accommodate the changing weather.

a bit out of the box

YARN: Blue Sky Alpacas, Alpaca (110 yards/50g ball)

FIBER CONTENT: 100% alpaca

COLORS: MC: 512; CC: 25

AMOUNT: MC: 9 (9, 10, 11); CC: 1 (1, 1, 1) balls

TOTAL YARDAGE: MC: 990 (990, 1100, 1210); CC: 110 (110, 110, 110) yards

STITCH GAUGE: 5¾ stitches = 1 inch; 23 stitches = 4 inches

ROW GAUGE: 8 rows = 1 inch; 32 rows = 4 inches

NEEDLE SIZE: U.S. #5 (3.75mm) for body or size needed to obtain gauge; U.S. #3 (3mm) for ribbing

SIZES: XS (S, M, L)

KNITTED MEASUREMENTS: Width = 16" (17", 18½", 20"); Length = 21" (22", 23", 24"); Sleeve Length = 16½" (17", 18", 19")

OTHER MATERIALS: 8 (9, 9, 9) buttons

Anne wanted to knit a warm but lightweight sweater for the fall. She wanted to do it only in stockinette stitch—so she wouldn't have to concentrate too much on her knitting once the new TV season began—yet she wanted the sweater to be distinctive and interesting at the same time. We first suggested that she knit a simple funnel-neck sweater in a fun multicolored yarn. But Anne wanted a timeless look, "something classy and classic, yet a little bit out of the box." We thought long and hard about how to accomplish this and finally came up with this raglan sweater with a button band across the front sleeve seam knit in a contrasting color. Anne loved the idea and decided to use a beautiful alpaca yarn in scrumptious fall colors. She (and her remote) was finally ready for must-see TV.

BACK AND FRONT:

With #3 needle and **MC,** cast on 92 (98, 106, 114) stitches. Work in K2, P2 ribbing for 10 rows as follows: For XS: K2, P2 every row. For S, M, and L: **ROW 1:** K2 *(P2, K2)* to end. **ROW 2:** P2 *(K2, P2)* to end. Repeat rows 1 and 2 4 times more. Change to #5 needle and work in St st until piece measures 13" (13½", 14", 14½") from cast-on edge, ending with a WS row. SHAPE RAGLAN ARM-

HOLES: Bind off 3 stitches at the beginning of the next 2 rows. Then decrease 1 stitch at each edge, every 4th row 2 (3, 3, 2) times, and then every other row 27 (27, 30, 33) times until 28 (32, 34, 38) stitches remain. Bind off all stitches loosely.

SLEEVES:

With #3 needle and **MC,** cast on 48 (50, 52, 54) stitches. Work in K2, P2 ribbing

for 10 rows as follows: For XS and M: K2, P2 every row. For S and L: **ROW 1:** K2 *(P2, K2)* to end. **ROW 2:** P2 *(K2, P2)* to end. Repeat rows 1 and 2 4 times more. Change to #5 needle and work in St st. **AT THE SAME TIME,** increase one stitch at each edge, every 8th row 10 (9, 7, 8) times, and then every 6th row 6 (8, 12, 12) times until you have 80 (84, 90, 94) stitches. *Note: Increase, leaving 2 edge stitches on either side of work. This means you should knit 2 stitches,*

increase a stitch, knit to the last 2 stitches, increase a stitch, and then knit the remaining 2 stitches. Increasing like this makes it easier to sew up your seams. Continue in St st until sleeve measures 16½" (17", 18", 19") from cast-on edge, ending with a WS row. SHAPE RAGLAN SLEEVE: Bind off 3 stitches at the beginning of the next 2 rows. Then decrease 1 stitch at each edge, every 4th row 2 (3, 3, 2) times, and then every other row 27 (27, 30, 33) times until 16 (18, 18, 18) stitches remain. Bind off all stitches loosely.

FINISHING:

Sew raglan pieces together, except for the left front sleeve. With #3 needle and **MC**, beginning at left front neck, pick up 84 (96, 100, 108) stitches. Work back and forth in K2, P2 ribbing for 8 rows. Bind off loosely. With #3 needle and **CC**, beginning at the top of the open sleeve seam, pick up 58 (64, 70, 72) stitches. Work in K2, P2 ribbing for 5 rows as follows: For S and L: K2, P2 every row. For XS and M: **ROW 1:** K2 *(P2, K2)* to end. **ROW 2:** P2 *(K2, P2)* to end. On row 6,

bind off all stitches loosely. With #3 needle and **CC**, beginning at the bottom top of the open body raglan seam, pick up 58 (64, 70, 72) stitches. Work in K2, P2 ribbing for 2 rows. **BUTTONHOLE ROW:** Rib 3 (2, 2, 2), [YO, Rib 2tog, Rib 5 (5, 6, 6)] 7 (8, 8, 8) times, end rib 2tog, YO, Rib 4 (4, 2, 4). Work in K2, P2 ribbing for 2 rows. Bind off all stitches loosely. Sew down the bottom of the sleeve ribbing to armhole edge. Sew down the bottom of the raglan body ribbing on top of that. Sew on buttons.

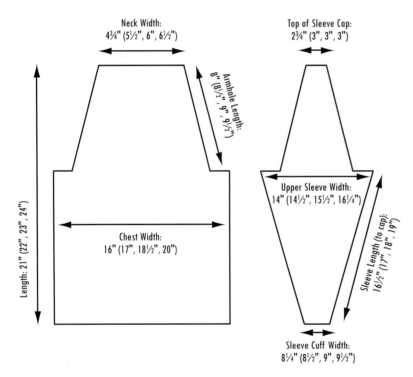

Neck Width:
4¾" (5½", 6", 6½")

Top of Sleeve Cap:
2¾" (3", 3", 3")

Armhole Length:
8" (8½", 9", 9½")

Length: 21" (22", 23", 24")

Chest Width:
16" (17", 18½", 20")

Upper Sleeve Width:
14" (14½", 15½", 16¼")

Sleeve Length (to cap):
16½" (17", 18", 19")

Sleeve Cuff Width:
8¼" (8½", 9", 9½")

olivia's sweatshirt

YARN: Crystal Palace Yarns, Merino Frappe (140 yards/50g ball)

FIBER CONTENT: 80% merino wool/20% polyamide

COLOR: 145

AMOUNT: 6 (6, 7, 8) balls

TOTAL YARDAGE: 840 (840, 980, 1120) yards

GAUGE: 4 stitches = 1 inch; 16 stitches = 4 inches

NEEDLE SIZE: U.S. #9 (5.5 mm) for body or size needed to obtain gauge; U.S. #7 (4.5mm) for ribbing

SIZES: XS (S, M, L)

KNITTED MEASUREMENTS: Width = 17" (18", 19", 20"); Length = 21" (22", 23", 23½"); Sleeve Length = 16½" (17½", 18", 19")

OTHER MATERIALS: 1 zipper

Olivia's uncle, Matt, bought her a toddler-sized warm-up suit featuring his favorite team's logo. One day, Julie dressed Olivia up in it and brought her to The Yarn Company. The adults thought that two-year-old Olivia looked pretty cute in the sweat suit. At some point, Julie and Jordana realized that the shape of the jacket could make a cute sweater for an adult. They designed this sweatshirt out of lightweight soft wool. It has a cozy feel and looks like a sweatshirt with a slightly more sophisticated appearance. They used their best judgment and decided not to knit the pants.

BACK:

With #7 needle, cast on 68 (72, 76, 80) stitches. Work in K2, P2 ribbing for 6 rows. Then change to #9 needle and work in St st until piece measures 13" (13½", 14", 14") from cast-on edge, ending with a WS row. SHAPE ARM-HOLES: Bind off 3 stitches at the beginning of the next 2 rows. Bind off 2 stitches at the beginning of the next 2 rows. Then decrease 1 stitch at each edge, every other row 3 (4, 4, 4) times until 52 (54, 58, 62) stitches remain. Continue to work in St st until piece measures 21" (22", 23", 23½") from cast-on edge, ending with a WS row. Bind off all stitches loosely.

POCKET LININGS: (MAKE 2)

With #9 needle, cast on 14 (14, 15, 16) stitches. Work in St st until piece measures 4" (4½", 5", 5½") from cast-on edge, ending with a WS row for the right pocket lining and a RS row for the left pocket lining. Place stitches on a holder.

FRONT: (MAKE 2, REVERSE SHAPING)

With #7 needle, cast on 34 (36, 38, 40) stitches. Work in K2, P2 ribbing for 6 rows as follows: For XS and M: ROW 1: K2 *(P2, K2)* to end. ROW 2: P2 *(K2, P2)* to end. Repeat rows 1 and 2 twice more. For S and L: K2, P2 every row. Change to #9 needle and work in St st until piece measures 4" (4½", 5", 5½") from cast-on edge, ending with a WS. * FOR RIGHT FRONT: Knit 22 (24, 24, 26) stitches. Put the remaining 12 (12, 14, 14) stitches on a holder. Continue working in St st on the 22 (24, 24, 26) stitches, while AT THE SAME TIME knitting the last 2 stitches together on every knit row 12 (12, 13, 14) times until 10 (12, 11, 12) stitches remain, ending with a RS row. Place these 10 (12, 11, 12) stitches on a holder. Then knit the first 13 (13, 14, 15) stitches of the pocket lining, knit the 14th (14th, 15th, 16th) stitch of the pocket lining together with the 1st stitch from the first holder. Continue to work these 25 (25, 28, 29) stitches in St

st until you have worked 24 (24, 26, 28) rows, ending with a RS row. **NEXT ROW:** Purl the 25th (25th, 28th, 29th) stitch together with the first stitch from the remaining holder and continue to purl across these stitches. Continue to work in St st on these 34 (36, 38, 40) stitches until piece measures 13" (13½", 14", 14") from cast-on edge, ending with a RS row. SHAPE ARMHOLES AS FOR BACK AT SIDE EDGE ONLY until 26 (27, 29, 31) stitches remain. Continue to work in St st until piece measures 18½" (19½", 20½", 21") from cast-on edge, ending with a WS row. SHAPE CREW NECK: At beginning of neck edge every other row, bind off 4 stitches 1 time, 3 stitches 1 time, 2 stitches 1 time, 1 stitch 2 (2, 3, 3) times. Continue to work in St st on remaining 15 (16, 17, 19) stitches until piece measures 21" (22", 23", 23½") from cast-on edge ending with a WS row. Bind off all stitches loosely.

*FOR LEFT FRONT: K12 (12, 14, 14) stitches. Put these stitches on a holder. Continue in St st on the remaining 22 (24, 24, 26) stitches, while **AT THE SAME TIME,** beginning with the next knit row, K2tog at the beginning of every knit row until 10 (12, 11, 12) stitches remain, ending with a WS row. Place these stitches on a holder. Purl the first 13 (13, 14, 15) stitches of the pocket lining, purl the 14th (14th, 15th, 16th) stitch of the pocket lining together with the 1st stitch from the first holder. Continue to work these 25 (25, 28, 29) stitches in St st until you have worked 24 (24, 26, 28) rows, ending with a WS row. **NEXT ROW:** Knit the 25th (25th, 28th, 29th) stitch together with the first stitch from the remaining holder and continue to knit across these stitches. Continue to work in St st on these 34 (36, 38, 40) stitches until piece measures 13" (13½", 14", 14") from cast-on edge, ending with a WS row.

SHAPE ARMHOLES AS FOR BACK AT SIDE EDGE ONLY until 26 (27, 29, 31) stitches remain. Continue to work in St st until piece measures 18½" (19½", 20½", 21") from cast-on edge, ending with a RS row. SHAPE CREW NECK: At beginning of neck edge every other row, bind off 4 stitches 1 time, 3 stitches 1 time, 2 stitches 1 time, and 1 stitch 2 (2, 3, 3) times. Continue to work in St st on remaining 15 (16, 17, 19) stitches until piece measures 21" (22", 23", 23½") from cast-on edge ending with a WS row. Bind off all stitches loosely.

SLEEVES:

With #7 needle, cast on 34 (34, 36, 38) stitches. Work in K2, P2 ribbing for 6 rows as follows: For XS, S, and L: **ROW 1:** K2 *(P2, K2)* to end. **ROW 2:** P2 *(K2, P2)* to end. Repeat rows 1 and 2 twice more. For M: K2, P2 every row. Change to # 9 needle and work in St st. **AT THE SAME TIME,** increase one stitch at each edge, every 8th row 5 (6, 6, 7) times, and every 6th row 6 (7, 8, 8) times until you have 56 (60, 64, 68) stitches. *Note: Increase leaving 2 edge stitches on either side. This means you should knit 2 stitches, increase a stitch, knit to the last 2 stitches, increase a stitch, and then knit the remaining 2 stitches. Increasing like this makes it easier to sew up your seams.* When sleeve measures 16½" (17½", 18", 19") from cast-on edge, ending with a WS row, SHAPE CAP: Bind off 3 stitches at the beginning of the next 2 rows. Bind off 2 stitches at the beginning of the next 2 rows. Then decrease 1 stitch at each edge, every other row 3 (4, 4, 4) times. Bind off 2 stitches at the beginning of the next 14 (16, 16, 18) rows until 12 (10, 14, 14) stitches remain. Bind off all stitches loosely.

HOOD:

With #9 needle, cast on 36 (38, 40, 42) stitches. Work in St st until piece measures 20" (21", 22", 23"). Bind off all stitches loosely.

FINISHING:

Sew shoulder seams together. Sew sleeves on. Sew up side and sleeve seams. Fold the hood in half and sew down the back side. Then attach the hood to the body of the sweater by sewing it around the back neck and down the front neck shaping.

FRONT AND HOOD BANDS: With a circular #7 needle and RS facing, pick up 242 (254, 266, 278) stitches up right front, hood and left front. Work in K2, P2 ribbing for 6 rows as follows: **ROW 1:** K2 *(P2, K2)* to end. **ROW 2:** P2 *(K2, P2)* to end. Bind off all stitches loosely.

POCKET BANDS: With a #7 needle and RS facing, pick up 28 (28, 30, 32) stitches. Work in K2, P2 ribbing as follows: For XS, S, and L: K2, P2 every row. For M: **ROW 1:** K2 *(P2, K2)* to end. **ROW 2:** P2 *(K2, P2)* to end. Repeat rows 1 and 2 twice more. Stitch sides of pocket bands down and sew down lining. Sew in zipper.

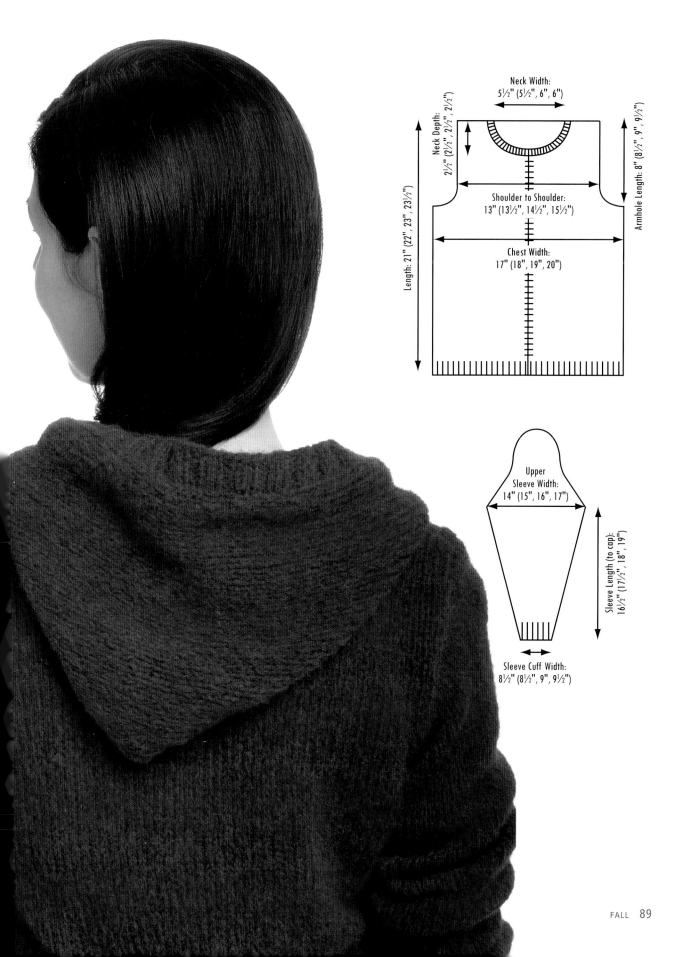

Neck Width:
5½" (5½", 6", 6")

Neck Depth:
2½" (2½", 2½", 2½")

Armhole Length: 8" (8½", 9", 9½")

Length: 21" (22", 23", 23½")

Shoulder to Shoulder:
13" (13½", 14½", 15½")

Chest Width:
17" (18", 19", 20")

Upper
Sleeve Width:
14" (15", 16", 17")

Sleeve Length (to cap):
16½" (17½", 18", 19")

Sleeve Cuff Width:
8½" (8½", 9", 9½")

the catwalk cable

YARN: Filatura di Crosa, Zara Plus (77 yards/50g ball)

FIBER CONTENT: 100% merino wool

COLOR: 19

AMOUNT: 11 (12, 14, 15) balls

TOTAL YARDAGE: 847 (924, 1078, 1155) yards

GAUGE: 4¾ stitches = 1 inch; 19 stitches = 4 inches (slightly stretched in cable pattern)

NEEDLE SIZE: U.S. #9 (5.5mm) for body or size needed to obtain gauge; U.S. #7 (4.5mm) for ribbing; 16" circular U.S. #7 (4.5mm) needle for neck band

SIZES: XS (S, M, L)

KNITTED MEASUREMENTS: Width = 16" (17", 18", 19"); Length = 21" (22", 23", 24"); Sleeve Length = 16½" (17", 18", 19")

It was fashion week in New York, and cabled sweaters were going to be hot this fall. Jill always kept up with the latest fashion trends, so we weren't surprised when she showed up at our store with a handful of tear sheets from all the latest fashion magazines. She wanted a great cabled sweater. Previously, Jill had only made cable sweaters with one cable up the center; she didn't want it to be too involved, but she did want numerous different cables. We designed this sweater for her. There are three basic cables throughout the sweater, so it's manageable. We set her up with some stitch markers, a row counter, and a cable needle and sent her on her way. The sweater came out great, and now Jill is making even the most complicated Aran patterns.

SPECIAL STITCHES:

C2F (Cable 2 into front): Slip 1 stitch to cable needle, hold at front, knit 1 stitch from left-hand needle, knit 1 from cable needle.

C2B (Cable 2 into back): Slip 1 stitch to cable needle, hold at back, knit 1 stitch from left-hand needle, knit 1 from cable needle.

C6B (Cable 6 into back): Slip 3 stitches to cable needle, hold at back, knit 3 stitches from left-hand needle, knit 3 stitches from cable needle.

PATTERN STITCHES:

FOR BACK AND FRONT:

ROW 1: P6 (9, 12, 15) *C2B, P2, C2F, C2B, P2, C2B, P2, K6, P2, C2B, P2, C2F, C2B, P2* repeat from * to * 1 more time, end C2B, P6 (9, 12, 15).

ROW 2: K6 (9, 12, 15) *P2, K2, P4, K2, P2, K2, P6, K2, P2, K2, P4, K2* repeat from * to * 1 more time, end P2, K6 (9, 12, 15).

ROW 3: P6 (9, 12, 15), *C2B, P2, K4, P2, C2B, P2, K6, P2, C2B, P2, K4, P2* repeat from * to * 1 more time, end C2B, P6 (9, 12, 15).

ROW 4: Same as row 2.

ROW 5: P6 (9, 12, 15) *C2B, P2, C2F, C2B, P2, C2B, P2, C6B, P2, C2B, P2, C2F, C2B, P2* repeat from * to * 1 more time, end C2B, P6 (9, 12, 15).

ROW 6: Same as row 2.

ROW 7: Same as row 3.

ROW 8: Same as row 2.

ROW 9: P6 (9, 12, 15) *C2B, P2, C2F, C2B, P2, C2B, P2, K6, P2, C2B, P2, C2F, C2B, P2* repeat from * to * 1 more time, end C2B, P6 (9, 12, 15).

ROW 10: Same as row 2.

ROW 11: P6 (9, 12, 15) *C2B, P2, K4, P2,

C2B, P2, C6B, P2, C2B, P2, K4, P2* repeat from * to * 1 more time, end C2B, P6 (9, 12, 15).

ROW 12: Same as row 2.

FOR SLEEVES:

ROW 1: P3 (4, 5, 6), C2B, P2, C2F, C2B, P2, C2B, P2, K6, P2, C2B, P2, C2F, C2B, P2, C2B, P3 (4, 5, 6).

ROW 2: K3 (4, 5, 6), P2, K2, P4, K2, P2, K2, P6, K2, P2, K2, P4, K2, P2, K3 (4, 5, 6).

ROW 3: P3 (4, 5, 6), C2B, P2, K4, P2, C2B, P2, K6, P2, C2B, P2, K4, P2, C2B, P3 (4, 5, 6).

ROW 4: Same as row 2.

ROW 5: P3 (4, 5, 6), C2B, P2, C2F, C2B, P2, C2B, P2, C6B, P2, C2B, P2, C2F, C2B, P2, C2B, P3 (4, 5, 6).

ROW 6: Same as row 2.

ROW 7: Same as row 3.

ROW 8: Same as row 2.

ROW 9: P3 (4, 5, 6), C2B, P2, C2F, C2B, P2, C2B, P2, K6, P2, C2B, P2, C2F, C2B, P2, C2B, P3 (4, 5, 6).

ROW 10: Same as row 2.

ROW 11: P3 (4, 5, 6), C2B, P2, K4, P2, C2B, P2, C6B, P2, C2B, P2, K4, P2, C2B, P3 (4, 5, 6).

ROW 12: Same as row 2.

BACK:

With #7 needle, cast on 78 (84, 90, 96) stitches. Work in K1, P1 ribbing for 6 rows. Change to #9 needle and work in pattern stitch until piece measures 13" (13½", 14", 15") from the cast-on edge, ending with a WS row. SHAPE ARM-HOLES: Bind off 3 stitches at the beginning of the next 2 rows. Bind off 2 stitches at the beginning of the following 2 rows. Then decrease 1 stitch at each edge, every other row 3 (4, 5, 6) times until 62 (66, 70, 74) stitches remain. Continue working in pattern stitch until piece measures 21" (22", 23", 24") from cast-on edge, ending with a WS row. Bind off all stitches loosely.

FRONT:

Work as for back until piece measures 13" (13½", 14", 15") from cast-on edge, ending with a WS row. SHAPE ARM-HOLES: Bind off 3 stitches at the beginning of the next 2 rows. Bind off 2 stitches at the beginning of the following 2 rows. Then decrease 1 stitch at each edge, every other row 3 (4, 5, 6) times until 62 (66, 70, 74) stitches remain. Continue working in pattern stitch until piece measures 18½" (19½", 20½", 21½") from cast-on edge, ending with a WS row. SHAPE CREW NECK: Bind off center 12 (12, 14, 14) stitches and then begin working each side of the neck separately. At the beginning of each neck edge, every other row bind off 4 stitches 1 time, 3 stitches 1 time, 2 stitches 1 time, and 1 stitch 2 (2, 2, 3) times. Continue to work on remaining 14 (16, 17, 18) stitches with no further decreasing until piece measures 21" (22", 23", 24") from cast-on edge, ending with a WS row. Bind off all stitches loosely.

SLEEVES:

With #7 needle, cast on 40 (42, 44, 46) stitches. Work in K1, P1 ribbing for 6 rows. Change to #9 needle and work in pattren stitch. **AT THE SAME TIME,** increase 1 stitch at each edge, every 8th row 11 (12, 13, 15) times until you have 62 (66, 70, 76) stitches. *Note: Increase leaving 2 edge stitches on either side. This means you should work 2 stitches, increase a stitch, work to the last 2 stitches, increase a stitch, and then work the remaining 2 stitches. Increasing like this makes it easier to sew up your seams.* When sleeve measures 16½" (17", 18", 19") from cast-on edge, ending with a WS row, SHAPE CAP: Bind off 3 stitches at the beginning of the next 2 rows. Bind off 2 stitches at the beginning

of the next 2 rows. Then decrease 1 stitch at each edge, every other row 3 (4, 5, 6) times. Bind off 2 stitches at the beginning of the next 16 (18, 18, 20) rows until 14 (12, 14, 14) stitches remain. Bind off all stitches loosely.

FINISHING:

Sew shoulder seams together. Sew sleeves on. Then sew up side and sleeve seams.

With a circular 16" #7 needle, pick up 78 (78, 82, 86) stitches around neck and work in K1, P1 ribbing for 6 rows. Bind off all stitches loosely.

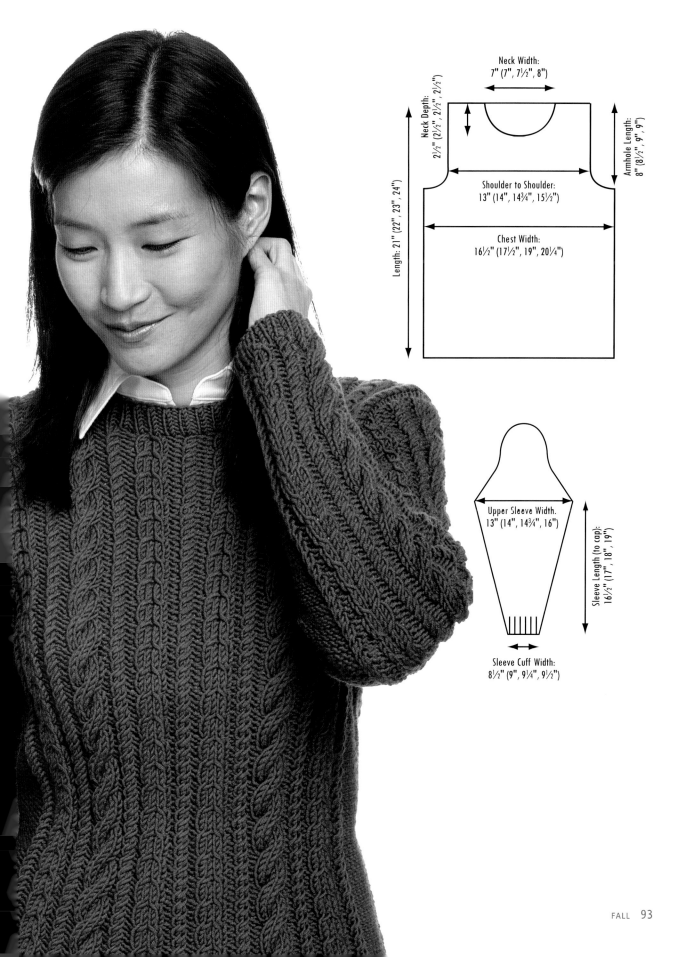

Neck Width:
7" (7", 7½", 8")

Neck Depth:
2½" (2½", 2½", 2½")

Armhole Length:
8" (8½", 9", 9")

Length: 21" (22", 23", 24")

Shoulder to Shoulder:
13" (14", 14¾", 15½")

Chest Width:
16½" (17½", 19", 20¼")

Upper Sleeve Width.
13" (14", 14¾", 16")

Sleeve Length (to cap):
16½" (17", 18", 19")

Sleeve Cuff Width:
8½" (9", 9¼", 9½")

the separation sweater

YARN: Ingeberg Michels, Naturwolle (110 yards /100g ball)

FIBER CONTENT: 100% wool

COLOR: 85

AMOUNT: 6 (6, 6, 7) balls

TOTAL YARDAGE: 660 (660, 660, 770) yards

GAUGE: 3 stitches = 1 inch; 12 stitches = 4 inches

NEEDLE SIZE: U.S. #11 (8mm) or size needed to obtain gauge, K (6.5mm) crochet hook

SIZES: XS (S, M, L)

KNITTED MEASUREMENTS: Width = 16 " (17½", 18½", 20"); Length = 22" (22½", 23", 24"); Sleeve Length = 17" (17½", 18", 19")

Jenny's son Jonathan was beginning preschool this fall. She was informed that "separation" could take up to three weeks and that the moms or dads bringing their child to school would first have to sit outside the classroom, in the hallway, and then in a conference room down the hall. After that they could leave the building and go sit in the coffee shop with their cell phones on until all the children were comfortable and okay. For Jenny, this was the perfect opportunity to get some serious knitting done. She came to the store wanting an easy sweater that would knit up quickly. It had to be something she didn't have to think about so that she could chat with the other parents at the same time. We thought this cute V-neck tie cardigan was perfect. It looks like there is an A-line shape to the body—but there isn't—and the bell sleeves are made by just knitting straight, with no increasing. Jonathan separated in two weeks, and Jenny had a great new sweater.

BACK:

With #11 needle, cast on 48 (52, 56, 60) stitches. Work in St st until piece measures 14" (14", 14", 14½") from cast-on edge, ending with a WS row. SHAPE ARMHOLES: FOR XS: Bind off 3 stitches at the beginning of the next 2 rows. Then decrease 1 stitch at each edge, every other row 2 times until 38 stitches remain. FOR S, M, and L: Bind off 3 stitches at the beginning of the next 2 rows. Bind off 2 stitches at the beginning of the following 2 rows. Then decrease 1 stitch at each edge, every other row 1 (2, 3) time(s) until 40 (42, 44) stitches remain. Continue to work in St st until piece measures 22" (22½", 23", 24") from cast-on edge, ending with a WS row. Bind off all stitches loosely.

FRONT: (MAKE 2, REVERSE SHAPING)

Note: You may be shaping the armhole and the V-neck at the same time. Please read the instructions before proceeding.

With #11 needle, cast on 24 (26, 28, 30) stitches. Work in St st until piece measures 14" (14", 14", 14½") from cast-on edge, ending with a WS row for the left front and a RS row for the right front. SHAPE ARMHOLES AS FOR BACK AT SIDE EDGE ONLY until 19 (20, 21, 22) stitches remain. Continue to work in St st until piece measures 15" (15", 15½", 16") from cast-on edge, ending with a RS row for the left front and a WS row for the right front. SHAPE V-NECK: For left front when worn: ROW 1: Knit until last 4 stitches, K2tog, K2. ROW 2: Purl. ROW 3: Knit. ROW 4: Purl. Repeat rows 1–4 1 more time. Then repeat rows 1 and 2 6 (7, 8, 8) more times. Continue to work on remaining 11 (11, 11, 12) stitches until piece measures 22" (22½", 23", 24") from cast-on edge, ending with a WS row. Bind off all stitches loosely. For right front when worn: ROW 1: K2, SSK, knit to end. ROW 2: Purl. ROW 3: Knit. ROW 4: Purl. Repeat rows 1–4 1 more time. Then repeat rows 1 and 2 6 (7, 8, 8) more times. Continue to work on remaining 11 (11, 11, 12) stitches until piece measures 22" (22½", 23", 24") from cast-on edge ending with a WS row. Bind off all stitches loosely.

SLEEVES:

With #11 needle, cast on 36 (38, 40, 42) stitches. Work in St st until piece measures 17" (17½", 18", 19") from cast-on edge, ending with a WS row. SHAPE CAP: FOR XS: Bind off 3 stitches at the beginning of the next 2 rows. Then decrease 1 stitch at each edge, every other row 2 times until 26 stitches remain. FOR S, M, and L: Bind off 3 stitches at the beginning of the next 2 rows. Bind off 2 stitches at the beginning of the following 2 rows. Then decrease 1 stitch at each edge, every other row 1 (2, 3) time(s) until 26 stitches remain. FOR ALL SIZES: Bind off 1 stitch at the begin-

ning of the next 16 rows until 10 stitches remain. Bind off all stitches loosely.

FINISHING:

Sew shoulder seams together. Sew sleeves on. Sew up side and sleeve seams. With a K crochet hook, work 1 row of single crochet around all edges. When working the single crochet up the fronts make 25 chain stitches where the V-neck begins on each side and single crochet back for ties.

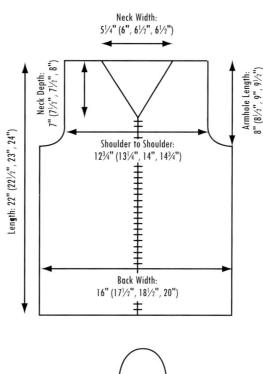

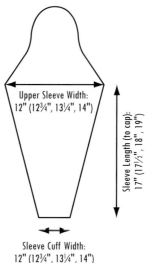

retro returns

YARN: Blue Sky Alpacas, Alpaca Worsted (100 yards/100g ball)

FIBER CONTENT: 50% alpaca/50% merino wool

COLOR: 2010

AMOUNT: 9 (10, 11, 12) balls

TOTAL YARDAGE: 900 (1000, 1100, 1200) yards

GAUGE: 3 stitches = 1 inch; 12 stitches = 4 inches

NEEDLE SIZE: U.S. #13 (9mm) for body or size needed to obtain gauge; U.S. #10 (6mm) for ribbing; 32" (80cm) circular U.S. #10 (6mm) for band; K (6.5mm) crochet hook

SIZES: XS (S, M, L)

KNITTED MEASUREMENTS: Width = 16½" (17½", 18½", 20"); Length = 22" (23", 24", 25"); Sleeve Length = 16½" (17", 18", 19")

Once again we were out on our annual survey of Madison Avenue stores to see what designers were showing on the sweater front for fall. The one resounding theme that we noticed was a look we thought had been left behind in the seventies (and no, it wasn't a poncho). The shawl-collared cardigan was back with a vengeance in the twenty-first century. Today's version was updated and much more sophisticated, and we loved it. We chose a beautiful alpaca/wool blend to make this jacket-like cardigan, and we knit it up a little loose to give it the perfect drape. The beautiful orange we chose reminded us of a wonderful fall day in the park when the leaves are at the peak of turning.

BACK:

With #10 needle, cast on 50 (52, 56, 60) stitches. Work in K2, P2 ribbing for 5" as follows: For XS: ROW 1: K2 *(P2, K2)* to end. ROW 2: P2 *(K2, P2)* to end. Repeat rows 1 and 2 until piece measures 5" from cast-on edge. For S, M, and L: K2, P2 every row until piece measures 5" from cast-on edge. Change to #13 needle and work in St st until piece measures 14" (14½", 15", 15½") from cast-on edge, ending with a WS row. S H A P E A R M H O L E S : Bind off 2 stitches at the beginning of the next 2 rows. Then decrease 1 stitch at each edge, every other row 4 (4, 5, 6) times until 38 (40,

42, 44) stitches remain. *Note: Work decreases as follows: K3, SSK, Knit until 5 stitches remain, K2tog, K3.* Continue to work in St st until piece measures 22" (23", 24", 25") from cast-on edge, ending with a WS row. Bind off all stitches loosely.

FRONT:

Note: You will be shaping the V-neck before you begin shaping the armholes. Please read the instructions before proceeding.

LEFT FRONT: (WHEN WORN) With #10 needle, cast on 24 (26, 28, 30) stitches. Work in K2, P2 ribbing for 5" as follows: For S and L: ROW 1: K2 *(P2, K2)* to end. ROW 2: P2 *(K2, P2)* to end. Repeat rows 1 and 2 until piece measures 5" from cast-on edge. For XS and M: K2, P2 every row until piece measures 5" from cast-on edge. Change to #13 needle and work in St st until piece measures 13" (13½", 14½", 15"), ending with a WS row. SHAPE V-NECK: ROW 1: Knit until last 4 stitches, K2tog, K2. ROW 2: Purl. ROW 3: Knit. ROW 4: Purl. Repeat rows 1–4 8 more times. **AT THE SAME TIME,** when piece measures 14" (14½", 15", 15½") from cast-on edge, ending with a WS row for the left front, SHAPE ARMHOLES AS FOR BACK AT SIDE EDGE ONLY.

When you are finished with the V-neck and armhole decreases, 9 (11, 12, 13) stitches should remain. Continue in St st until piece measures 22" (23", 24", 25") from cast-on edge, ending with a WS row. Bind off all stitches loosely.

RIGHT FRONT:
(WHEN WORN)

With #10 needle, cast on 24 (26, 28, 30) stitches. Work in K2, P2 ribbing for 5" as follows: For S and L: **ROW 1:** K2 *(P2, K2)* to end. **ROW 2:** P2 *(K2, P2)* to end. Repeat rows 1 and 2 until piece measures 5" from cast-on edge. For XS and M: K2, P2 every row until piece measures 5" from cast-on edge. Change to #13 needle and work in St st until piece measures 13" (13½", 14½", 15"), ending with a WS row. SHAPE V-NECK: **ROW 1:** K2, SSK, knit to end. **ROW 2:** Purl. **ROW 3:** Knit. **ROW 4:** Purl. Repeat rows 1–4 8 more times. **AT THE SAME TIME,** when piece measures 14" (14½", 15", 15½") from cast-on edge, ending with a RS row for the right front, SHAPE ARMHOLES AS FOR BACK AT SIDE EDGE ONLY. When you are finished with the V-neck and armhole decreases, 9 (11, 12, 13) stitches should remain. Continue in St st until piece measures 22" (23", 24", 25") from cast-on edge, ending with a WS row. Bind off all stitches loosely.

SLEEVES:

With #10 needle, cast on 26 (28, 30, 32) stitches. Work in K2, P2 ribbing for 6" as follows: For XS and M: **ROW 1:** K2 *(P2, K2)* to end. **ROW 2:** P2 *(K2, P2)* to end. Repeat rows 1 and 2 until piece measures 6" from cast-on edge. For S and L: K2, P2 every row until piece measures 6" from cast-on edge. Change to #13 needles and work in St st. **AT THE SAME TIME,** increase 1 stitch at each edge, every 8th row 4 (4, 5, 5) times and then every 6th row 2 times until you have 38 (40, 44, 46) stitches. *Note: Increase leaving 2 edge stitches on either side. This means you should knit 2 stitches, increase a stitch, knit to the last 2 stitches, increase a stitch, and then knit the remaining 2 stitches. Increasing like this makes it easier to sew up your seams.* When sleeve measures 16½" (17", 18", 19") from cast-on edge, ending with a WS row, SHAPE CAP: Bind off 2 stitches at the beginning of the next 2 rows. Then decrease 1 stitch at each edge, every other row 4 (4, 5, 6) times. Bind off 2 stitches at the beginning of the next 10 (10, 12, 12) rows until 6 (8, 6, 6) stitches remain. Bind off all stitches loosely.

FINISHING:

Sew shoulder seams together. Sew sleeves on. Sew up side and sleeve seams. At side edges, right above ribbing, using a K crochet hook, make a belt loop by chaining 6 stitches.
With a 32" circular #10 needle and WS facing, pick up 64 (68, 72, 76) stitches up the right front to beginning of V-neck shaping, place marker (pm), pick up 34 (36, 38, 40) stitches up right neck, pm, pick up 20 (20, 20, 20) stitches across back neck, pm, pick up 34 (36, 38, 40) down left neck to end of V-neck shaping, pm, pick up 64 (68, 72, 76) stitches down left front. You will have 216 (228, 240, 252) stitches. Work in K2, P2 ribbing for 8". Bind off all stitches loosely.

BELT:

With #10 needle, cast on 16 stitches. Work in St st for 60" (60", 64", 68"). Bind off. Fold in half lengthwise and sew down.

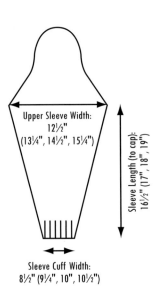

Upper Sleeve Width:
12½"
(13¼", 14½", 15¼")

Sleeve Length (to cap):
16½" (17", 18", 19")

Sleeve Cuff Width:
8½" (9¼", 10", 10½")

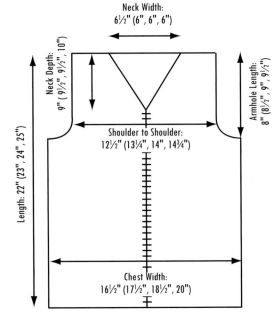

Neck Width:
6½" (6", 6", 6")

Neck Depth:
9" (9½", 9½", 10")

Armhole Length:
8" (8½", 9", 9½")

Length: 22" (23", 24", 25")

Shoulder to Shoulder:
12½" (13¼", 14", 14¾")

Chest Width:
16½" (17½", 18½", 20")

a worthwhile investment

YARN: Filatura di Crosa, Zara (136.5 yards/50g ball)

FIBER CONTENT: 100% merino wool

COLORS: A: 1523; B: 1022; C: 1461; D: 1451

AMOUNT: A: 3 (3, 4, 4); B: 2 (2, 3, 3); C: 1 (1, 1, 1); D: 1(1, 1, 1) balls

TOTAL YARDAGE: A: 408 (408, 546, 546); B: 272 (272, 408, 408); C: 136 (136, 136, 136); D: 136 (136, 136, 136) yards

GAUGE: 5 stitches = 1 inch; 20 stitches = 4 inches

NEEDLE SIZE: U.S. #7 (4.5mm) for body or size needed to obtain gauge; U.S. #5 (3.75mm) for ribbing; 16" circular U.S. #5 (3.75mm) for neck ribbing

SIZES: XS (S, M, L)

KNITTED MEASUREMENTS: Width = 15$^1/_2$" (16$^1/_2$", 18", 19"); Length = 21" (21$^1/_2$", 22", 23")

Jordana's friend Debra frequently wore a collared shirt with a V-neck vest. Jordana always thought it looked nerdy. After a while, however, the look started to grow on her, and she decided to go buy herself a vest. But she couldn't find one that she really liked, so she decided to knit one. She jazzed it up by adding all kinds of stripes. Jordana was so happy that she finally saw the light. Not only did she like the look of the vest, but the vest provided the perfect amount of warmth on cool fall days. This project turned out to be a worthwhile investment.

STRIPE PATTERN:

The stripe pattern is worked in St st thoughout.

2 ROWS B
1 ROW C
1 ROW D
1 ROW C
2 ROWS A
1 ROW C
1 ROW D
1 ROW C
2 ROWS B
2 ROWS A
1 ROW D
2 ROWS A

BACK:

With #5 needle and **color A,** cast on 78 (84, 90, 96) stitches. Work in K2, P2 ribbing for 6 rows as follows: For XS and M: **ROW 1:** K2 *(P2, K2)* to end. **ROW 2:** P2 *(K2, P2)* to end. Repeat rows 1 and 2 twice more. For S and L: K2, P2 every row. Change to #7 needle and work in striped St st until piece measures 13$^1/_2$" (13$^1/_2$", 13$^1/_2$", 14") from cast-on edge, ending with a WS row. S H A P E A R M H O L E S : Bind off 4 stitches at the beginning of the next 2 rows. Bind off 3 stitches at the beginning of the next 2 rows. Bind off 2 stitches at the beginning of the next 2 rows. Then

decrease 1 stitch at each edge, every other row 1 (2, 2, 3) time(s) until 58 (62, 68, 72) stitches remain. Continue working in striped St st until piece measures 21" (21$^1/_2$", 22", 23") from cast-on edge, ending with a WS row. Bind off all stitches loosely.

FRONT:

Note: You may be shaping the armhole and the V-neck at the same time. Please read the instructions before proceeding.

With #5 needle and **color A** cast on 78 (84, 90, 96) stitches. Work as for back until piece measures 13$^1/_2$" (13$^1/_2$", 13$^1/_2$",

14") from cast-on edge, ending with a WS row. SHAPE ARMHOLES: Bind off 4 stitches at the beginning of the next 2 rows. Bind off 3 stitches at the beginning of the next 2 rows. Bind off 2 stitches at the beginning of the next 2 rows. Then decrease 1 stitch at each edge, every other row 1 (2, 2, 3) time(s) until 58 (62, 68, 72) stitches remain. Continue working in striped St st until piece measures 14" (14", 14", 14½") from cast-on edge, ending with a WS row. SHAPE V-NECK: Place a marker at the center. ROW 1: Knit until 4 stitches before the marker, K2tog, K2. Turn work around as if you were at the end of the row. Ignore the rest of the stitches. ROW 2: Purl. ROW 3: Knit. ROW 4: Purl. Repeat rows 1–4 5 (5, 5, 6) more times until 23 (25, 28, 29) stitches remain. Then repeat rows 1 and 2 8 (9, 9, 9) times until 15 (16, 19, 20) stitches remain. Continue to work on these stitches until piece measures 21" (21½", 22", 23") from cast-on edge, ending with a WS row. Bind off remaining stitches loosely. Attach yarn to other side. You should be on a RS row. ROW 1: K2, SSK, knit until end. ROW 2: Purl. ROW 3: Knit. ROW 4: Purl. Repeat rows 1–4 5 (5, 5, 6) more times until 23 (25, 28, 29) stitches remain. Then repeat rows 1 and 2 8 (9, 9, 9) times until 15 (16, 19, 20) stitches remain. Continue to work on these stitches until piece measures 21" (21½", 22", 23") from cast-on edge, ending with a WS row. Bind off remaining stitches loosely.

FINISHING:

Sew shoulder seams together. Sew down side seams. V-NECK RIBBING: With a 16" #5 circular needle, pick up 34 (34, 38, 38) stitches across the back neck, 56 (60, 66, 68) stitches down the left front, 1 stitch in the center of the V, 56 (60, 66, 68) stitches up the right neck. You should have 147 (155, 171, 175) stitches. Work in K2, P2 ribbing, keeping the center stitch as a knit 1 and decreasing 1 stitch before the knit 1 by doing a K2tog and 1 stitch after the knit 1 by doing an SSK. Work 5 rows in the ribbing with the decreases and then bind off loosely.

ARMHOLE RIBBINGS:
With a 16" #5 circular needle, pick up 106 (110, 118, 122) stitches around armhole. Work in K2, P2 ribbing for 5 rows. Bind off loosely.

Note: If you end with a K2 before the center stitch, begin with a K2 up the right side. If you end with a P2 before the center stitch, begin with a P2 up the right side.

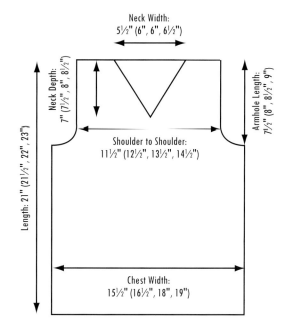

Neck Width:
5½" (6", 6", 6½")

Neck Depth:
7" (7½", 8", 8½")

Armhole Length:
7½" (8", 8½", 9")

Length: 21" (21½", 22", 23")

Shoulder to Shoulder:
11½" (12½", 13½", 14½")

Chest Width:
15½" (16½", 18", 19")

a change of pace

YARN: A, B, and C: GGH, Soft Kid (145 yards/25g ball); D: Tahki Select, Flower (38 yards/25g ball)

FIBER CONTENT: A, B, C: 70% super kid mohair/25% polyamide/5% wool; D: 25% sinflex/35% tactel/40% polyester

COLORS: A: 77; B: 73; C: 55; D: 9

AMOUNT: 1 ball each color A, B, C, D

GAUGE: 4 stitches = 1 inch; 16 stitches = 4 inches

NEEDLE SIZE: U.S. #9 (5.5 mm) or size needed to obtain gauge

SIZES: One size

KNITTED MEASUREMENTS: Width = 3"; Length = 40"

Garter stitch is a great scarf stitch. It's quick and it's reversible. It was Joanne's favorite stitch. Actually, it was the only stitch Joanne knew, and she was not interested in learning another. For a change of pace, we decided that she should cast on lengthwise and knit for about 3". We also suggested striping the scarf; when a scarf is knit lengthwise, you end up with vertical stripes instead of horizontal ones, which is a nice change. It looked great when she was done, but something was missing. We suggested she pick another fun yarn and pick up stitches at either end and do some seed stitch. She agreed and begrudgingly learned to purl so she could do seed stitch. In the end, Joanne was thrilled. Not only had she finally learned to purl, but she now had a fabulous scarf that she got compliments on wherever she went.

STRIPE PATTERN:

The stripe pattern is worked in garter stitch.

2 rows A
2 rows B
2 rows C
2 rows B
2 rows A
2 rows B
2 rows C
2 rows B

SCARF:

With #9 needle and **color A,** cast on 160 stitches. Work stripe pattern. Bind off loosely with A.

Then at each end, with #9 needle and 1 strand of **color D,** with RS facing, pick up 11 stitches. Work in seed stitch for 2¹/₂". Bind off loosely.

dori's a genius

Customers often come into our store and ask us whether we have a pattern for fingerless gloves. While there are patterns out there, many require the use of double-pointed needles or some other slightly complicated maneuvering that some knitters tend to shy away from. So when we were out one night with Dori, who used to work for us, and she asked, "Have you made these yet?"—showing us a pair of fingerless gloves—we said no and *oohed* and *ahhed* a bit. Dori then told us that they were the simplest thing ever: "Just knit up a rectangle and sew up the seam, leaving a hole for the thumb." Genius! We decided that these would be perfect for the book and added a little ruffle of our own for good measure—but we really have to thank Dori for the great, simple idea!

GLOVES:

With #9 needle and 2 strands of yarn, cast on 72 stitches. Work 2 rows in garter. Work 3rd row as follows: K2tog across row. Beginning with a knit row, continue to work in St st on remaining 36 stitches until piece measures 8" from cast on. Bind off all stitches loosely.

FINISHING:

Sew down seams, leaving a space for your thumb.

the nonconformist

YARN: Filatura di Crosa, Zara Plus (77 yards/50g ball)

FIBER CONTENT: 100% merino wool

COLORS: A: 405; B: 14

AMOUNT: A: 8 (9, 10, 11); B: 5 (6, 7, 8) balls

TOTAL YARDAGE: A: 616 (693, 770, 847); B: 385 (462, 539, 616) yards

GAUGE: 4 stitches = 1 inch; 16 stitches = 4 inches

NEEDLE SIZE: U.S. #10 (6mm) for body or size needed to obtain gauge; U.S. #8 (5mm) for ribbing; circular 16" U.S. #8 (5mm) needle for neck ribbing

SIZES: S (M, L, XL)

KNITTED MEASUREMENTS: Width = 22" (23½", 25", 26"); Length = 23" (24", 25" 26"); Sleeve Length = 18" (19", 19½", 20")

Julie's husband, John, always likes to be a little different. He practices Bagua Zhang, not a more common martial art like tai chi or karate. At a restaurant he will order the rabbit, squab, or frog's legs, but not the chicken or the steak. And he knows the oddest factoids found in the hidden depths of Internet research. He is consistent in his quirkiness, even when it comes to the sweaters Julie makes for him. No plain pullover sweaters for him—he always wants something a little out of the ordinary. One day, while trying to decide on a sweater to make for John, Julie came up with this idea for a two-tone saddle shoulder sweater. It was perfect. The saddle shoulder style was just eclectic enough so that John felt his sweater was separated from the masses.

BACK:

With #8 needle and **color A,** cast on 88 (94, 100, 104) stitches. Work in K1, P1 ribbing for 6 rows. Change to #10 needle and work in St st until piece measures 14" (14½", 15", 16") from the cast-on edge, ending with a WS row. SHAPE ARMHOLES: Bind off 4 stitches at the beginning of the next 2 rows. Bind off 3 stitches at the beginning of the following 2 rows. Bind off 2 stitches at the beginning of the next 2 rows. Then decrease 1 stitch at each edge 1 time until 68 (74, 80, 84) stitches remain. Continue working in St st until piece measures 21" (22", 23", 24") from cast-on edge, ending with a WS row. Bind off 19 (21, 24, 25) stitches at the beginning of the next 2 rows. Continue to work in St st on the remaining 30 (32, 32, 34) stitches until piece measures 23" (24", 25", 26") from cast-on edge, ending with a WS row. Bind off all stitches loosely.

FRONT:

Work as for back until piece measures 14" (14½", 15", 16") from cast-on edge, ending with a WS row. SHAPE ARMHOLES: Bind off 4 stitches at the beginning of the next 2 rows. Bind off 3 stitches at the beginning of the following 2 rows. Bind off 2 stitches at the beginning of the next 2 rows. Then decrease 1 stitch at each edge 1 time until 68 (74, 80, 84) stitches remain. Continue working in St st until piece measures 20½" (21½", 22½", 23½") from cast-on edge, ending with a WS row. SHAPE CREW NECK: Bind off center 14 (16, 16, 18) stitches and then begin working each side of the neck separately. At the beginning of

each neck edge, every other row bind off 3 stitches 1 time, 2 stitches 1 time, 1 stitch 3 times. When piece measures 21" (22", 23", 24") from cast-on edge, ending with a WS row, bind off remaining 19 (21, 24, 25) stitches loosely.

SLEEVES:

With #8 needle and **color B,** cast on 36 (38, 40, 40) stitches. Work in K1, P1 ribbing for 6 rows. Change to #10 needle and work in St st. **AT THE SAME TIME,** increase one stitch at each edge, every 6th row 14 (14, 14, 15) times until you have 64 (66, 68, 70) stitches. *Note: Increase leaving 2 edge stitches on either side. This means you should knit 2 stitches, increase a stitch, knit to the last 2 stitches, increase a stitch, and then knit the remaining 2 stitches. Increasing like this makes it easier to sew up your seams.* When sleeve measures 18" (19", 19½", 20") from cast-on edge, ending with a WS row, S H A P E C A P : Bind off 4 stitches at the beginning of the next 2 rows. Bind off 3 stitches at the beginning of the next 2 rows. Bind off 2 stitches at the beginning of the next 2 rows. Then decrease 1 stitch at each edge 1 time. Bind off 2 stitches at the beginning of the next 14 (14, 16, 16) rows until 16 (18, 16, 18) stitches remain. Work in St st on the remaining stitches for 4¾" (5¼", 6", 6¼") more. Bind off all stitches loosely.

FINISHING:

Sew saddle shoulder seams to corresponding front and back shoulder seams together. Then sew up side and sleeve seams.

With a circular 16" #8 needle and **color B,** pick up 72 (74, 76, 80) stitches around neck and work in K1, P1 ribbing for 6 rows. Bind off all stitches loosely.

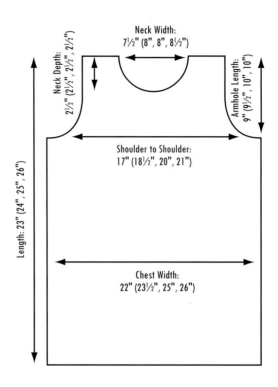

Neck Width:
7½" (8", 8", 8½")

Neck Depth:
2½" (2½", 2½", 2½")

Armhole Length:
9" (9½", 10", 10")

Length: 23" (24", 25", 26")

Shoulder to Shoulder:
17" (18½", 20", 21")

Chest Width:
22" (23½", 25", 26")

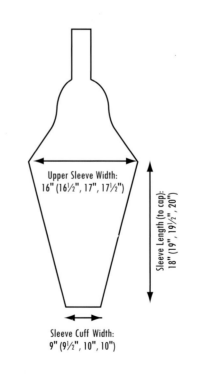

Upper Sleeve Width:
16" (16½", 17", 17½")

Sleeve Length (to cap):
18" (19", 19½", 20")

Sleeve Cuff Width:
9" (9½", 10", 10")

the fashionista

YARN: Blue Sky Alpacas, Alpaca (110 yards/50g ball)

FIBER CONTENT: 100% alpaca

COLORS: MC: 12; CC: 403

AMOUNT: MC: 13 (14, 15, 16); CC: 1 (1, 2, 2) balls

TOTAL YARDAGE: MC: 1430 (1540, 1650, 1760); CC: 110 (110, 220, 220) yards

GAUGE: 5¼ stitches = 1 inch; 21 stitches = 4 inches

NEEDLE SIZE: U.S. #6 (4mm) for body or size needed to obtain gauge; U.S. #4 (3.5mm) for ribbing

SIZES: S (M, L, XL)

KNITTED MEASUREMENTS: Width = 21" (22½", 24", 25"); Length = 23" (24", 25", 26"); Sleeve Length = 18" (19", 19½", 20")

Carly's husband, Bob, is a bit of a male fashionista. He recently went shopping at an upscale men's clothing store in the hope of updating his fall wardrobe. He fell in love with a handsome cashmere polo collar sweater. The price tag was a bit too much—even for him—so he sent Carly into our store with a sketch of this much-coveted sweater so we could recreate it. We also had the following guidelines to work with: the yarn must be soft, like cashmere, it must be lightweight, and the main color should be classic while the contrasting color should add a little interest. This was a tall order to fill, but we chose an alpaca yarn that is lightweight and super soft. The charcoal color couldn't be more classic, and the contrasting color for the bottom edges and inside of the polo collar adds just the right amount of whimsy. Bob wears it every chance he gets.

BACK:

With #4 needle and **CC,** cast on 110 (118, 126, 130) stitches. Work in K1, P1 ribbing for 2 rows. Change to **MC** and work in K1, P1 ribbing for 8 more rows. Change to #6 needle and work in St st until piece measures 14" (14½", 15½", 16") from the cast-on edge, ending with a WS row. SHAPE ARMHOLES: Bind off 4 stitches at the beginning of the next 2 rows. Bind off 3 stitches at the beginning of the next 2 rows. Bind off 2 stitches at the beginning of the next 2 rows. Then decrease 1 stitch at each edge, every other row 4 (4, 4, 3) times until 84 (92, 100, 106) stitches remain. Continue working in St st until piece measures 23" (24", 25", 26") from cast-on edge, ending with a WS row. Bind off all stitches loosely.

FRONT:

Note: You may be shaping the armhole and the V-neck at the same time. Please read the instructions before proceeding.

Work as for back until piece measures 14" (14½", 15½", 16") from cast-on edge, ending with a WS row. SHAPE ARMHOLES: Bind off 4 stitches at the beginning of the next 2 rows. Bind off 3 stitches at the beginning of the next 2 rows. Bind off 2 stitches at the beginning of the next 2 rows. Then decrease 1 stitch at each edge, every other row 4 (4, 4, 3) times until 84 (92, 100, 106) stitches remain. Continue working in St st until piece measures 15" (16", 17", 17½") from cast-on edge, ending with a WS row. SHAPE PLACKET: Bind off center 4 (4, 6, 6) stitches. Continue working each side separately until piece measures 20½" (21½", 22½", 23½") and then SHAPE NECK: At the beginning of each neck edge, every other row bind off 5 stitches 1 time, 4 stitches 1 time, 3 stitches 1 time, 2 stitches 1 time, and 1 stitch 1 (1, 2, 2) time(s). Continue to work on remaining 25 (29, 31, 34) stitches with no further decreasing until piece measures 23" (24", 25", 26") from cast-on edge, ending with a WS row. Bind off all stitches loosely.

SLEEVES:

With #4 needle and **CC,** cast on 48 (52, 56, 56) stitches. Work in K1, P1 ribbing for 2 rows. Change to **MC** and work in K1, P1 ribbing for 8 more rows. Change to #6 needle and work in St st. **AT THE SAME TIME,** increase 1 stitch at each edge, every 8th row 0 (6, 6, 4) times and every 6th row 18 (11, 11, 15) times until you have 84 (86, 90, 94) stitches. *Note: Increase leaving 2 edge stitches on either side. This means you should knit 2 stitches, increase a stitch, knit to the last 2 stitches, increase a stitch, and then knit the remaining 2 stitches. Increasing like this makes it easier to sew up your seams.* When sleeve measures 18" (19", 19½", 20") from cast-on edge, ending with a WS row, SHAPE CAP: Bind off 4 stitches at the beginning of the next 2 rows. Bind off 3 stitches at the beginning of the next 2 rows. Bind off 2 stitches at the beginning of the next 2 rows. Then decrease 1 stitch at each edge, every other row 4 (4, 4, 3) times. Bind off 2 stitches at the beginning of the next 20 (22, 24, 26) rows until 18 (16, 16, 18) stitches remain. Bind off all stitches loosely.

FINISHING:

Sew shoulder seams together. Sew sleeves on. Then sew up side and sleeve seams. With #4 needle and **CC,** pick up 32 (32, 32, 36) stitches up the right side placket. Work in K1, P1 ribbing for 10 rows. Bind off all stitches loosely. With #4 needle and CC, pick up 32 (32, 32, 36) stitches up the left side placket. Work in K1, P1 ribbing for 4 rows. Work buttonhole row as follows: (K1, P1) 3 times *K2tog, YO, rib 8 (8, 8 10)* repeat from * to * 1 more time, end K2tog, YO, (K1, P1) twice. Work 4 more rows in K1, P1 ribbing. Bind off all stitches loosely. With a #4 needle and **MC,** pick up 96 (96, 100, 100) stitches around neck and work in K1, P1 ribbing for 19 rows. Then work 1 row in purl. Change to **CC** and work 19 rows in K1, P1 ribbing. Bind off all stitches loosely. Fold in half and sew down to inside of neck.

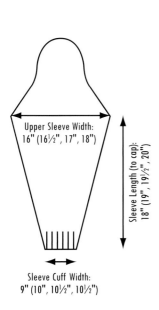

Upper Sleeve Width: 16" (16½", 17", 18")

Sleeve Length (to cap): 18" (19", 19½", 20")

Sleeve Cuff Width: 9" (10", 10½", 10½")

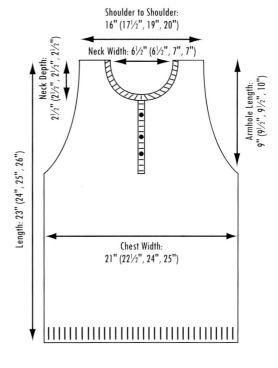

Shoulder to Shoulder: 16" (17½", 19", 20")

Neck Width: 6½" (6½", 7", 7")

Neck Depth: 2½" (2½", 2½", 2½")

Armhole Length: 9" (9½", 9½", 10")

Length: 23" (24", 25", 26")

Chest Width: 21" (22½", 24", 25")

winter

Winter is the season of blustery wind, crackling fires, frost-sparkled windows, and dark skies. In other words, winter is the perfect season for curling up on the couch under a warm blanket to knit.

The projects in this chapter focus on the combination of warmth, style, and holiday cheer. The fibers we've chosen are soft, comfortable, and, most importantly, warm. Many are also lightweight, so you won't feel so bogged down with all your other winter gear on. We've used merino wools, which are easy to wear and delightful to knit with, and we found a yak/merino blend that is warm, soft, and spongy. We've also decided to focus on warm tones to contrast the often overcast skies of the season. These colors made us feel cozy and comfy just looking at them. You will also find a few dressier items perfect for holidays parties.

better than the real deal

YARN: Karabella, Superyak (125 yards/ 50g ball)

FIBER CONTENT: 50% yak/50% merino wool

COLOR: 10203

AMOUNT: 6 (6, 7, 7) balls

TOTAL YARDAGE: 750 (750, 875, 875) yards

GAUGE: 3¾ stitches = 1 inch; 15 stitches = 4 inches

NEEDLE SIZE: U.S. #10½ (7mm) for body or size needed to obtain gauge; U.S. #9 (5.5mm) for ribbing

SIZES: XS (S, M, L)

KNITTED MEASUREMENTS: Width = 16½" (17¾", 18¾", 19¾"); Length = 22" (22½", 23", 23½"); Sleeve Length = 17½" (18", 18", 18½")

Shawl collars were back. They were in all the stores, and our customers kept asking for patterns. We kept directing them to patterns from books, because we hadn't written a pattern for this type of sweater. One day, Rosy, our editor, asked us for a pattern with a shawl collar for which she sketched a picture. We did not want to disappoint her, but we had very little experience with short-row shaping, a technique needed to knit shawl collars. Then, inspiration hit—we asked ourselves, What if we just have her pick up stitches and knit a large collar without short rows? We told her the collar would be shawl collarlike, only simpler to knit. Rosy was willing to experiment, so we wrote her this pattern. We recommended a yak/merino wool blend to create a soft and spongy sweater. After knitting it, she told us, "I love it even more than the real deal."

BACK:

With #10½ needle, cast on 62 (66, 70, 74) stitches. Work in St st until piece measures 14" (14", 14½", 14½") from cast-on edge, ending with a WS row.

SHAPE ARMHOLES: Bind off 3 stitches at the beginning of the next 2 rows. Bind off 2 stitches at the beginning of the next 2 rows. Then decrease 1 stitch at each edge, every other row 2 (2, 3, 4) times until 48 (52, 54, 56) stitches remain. Continue working in St st until piece measures 22" (22½", 23", 23½") from cast-on edge, ending with a WS row. Bind off all stitches loosely.

FRONT:

Note: You will begin shaping your neck before you shape your armholes. Please read the pattern before proceeding.

With #10½ needle, cast on 62 (66, 70, 74) stitches. Work in St st until piece measures 11" (11½", 12", 12½") from cast-on edge, ending with a WS row. SHAPE NECK: Bind off center 14 stitches and then begin working each side of the neck separately. At the beginning of each neck edge, every 6th row decrease 1 stitch 9 times. Work decreases as follows: For decreases on the right side (as you wear the garment) K2, SSK, knit to end. For decreases on the left side, knit until last 4 stitches, K2tog, K2. **AT THE SAME TIME** when piece measures 14" (14", 14½", 14½") from cast-on edge, ending with a WS row, SHAPE ARMHOLES at outside edges only as for back. Continue to work on remaining 8 (10, 11, 12) stitches with no further decreasing until piece measures 22" (22½", 23", 23½") from cast-on edge, ending with a WS row. Bind off all stitches loosely.

SLEEVES:

With #10½ needle, cast on 30 (32, 34, 36) stitches. Work in St st. **AT THE SAME TIME** increase one stitch at each edge, every 8th row 10 times until you have 50 (52, 54, 56) stitches. *Note: Increase leaving 2 edge stitches on either side of work. This means you should knit 2 stitches, increase a stitch, knit to the last 2 stitches, increase a stitch, and then knit the remaining 2 stitches. Increasing like this makes it easier to sew up your seams.* Continue in St st until sleeve measures 17½" (18", 18", 18½") from cast-on edge, ending with a WS row. SHAPE CAP: Bind off 3 stitches at the beginning of the next 2 rows. Bind off 2 stitches at the beginning of the next 2 rows. Then decrease 1 stitch at each

edge, every other row 2 (2, 3, 4) times. Bind off 2 stitches at the beginning of the next 14 rows. Bind off remaining 8 (10, 10, 10) stitches loosely.

FINISHING:

Sew shoulder seams together. Sew sleeves on. Then sew up side and sleeve seams. With a #9 needle, beginning at right side of center 14 bound-off stitches, pick up 50 stitches up right front, 34 across back neck, and 50 down left front. You will have 134 stitches. Work in K2, P2 ribbing for 24 rows. Bind off all stitches loosely. Sew the loose edge of the left neck band to where the 14 stitches were bound off. Sew the loose edge of the right neck band over that.

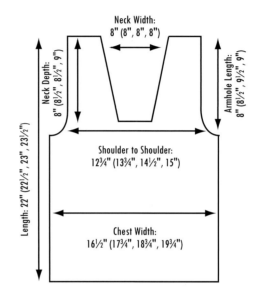

Neck Width:
8" (8", 8", 8")

Neck Depth:
8" (8½", 8½", 9")

Armhole Length:
8" (8½", 9½", 9")

Length: 22" (22½", 23", 23½")

Shoulder to Shoulder:
12¾" (13¾", 14½", 15")

Chest Width:
16½" (17¾", 18¾", 19¾")

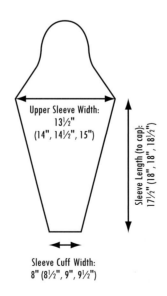

Upper Sleeve Width:
13½"
(14", 14½", 15")

Sleeve Length (to cap):
17½" (18", 18", 18½")

Sleeve Cuff Width:
8" (8½", 9", 9½")

now or never

YARN: Blue Sky Alpaca, Alpaca Worsted (100 yards/100g ball)

FIBER CONTENT: 50% alpaca/50% wool

COLOR: 2000

AMOUNT: 7 (8, 9, 10) balls

TOTAL YARDAGE: 700 (800, 900, 1000) yards

GAUGE: 3$^1/_2$ stitches = 1 inch; 14 stitches = 4 inches in stockinette stitch on #10 needles
4 stitches = 1 inch; 16 stitches = 4 inches in K2, P2 ribbing for sleeves on #8 needle

NEEDLE SIZE: U.S. #10 (6mm) for body or size needed to obtain gauge; U.S. #8 (5mm) for ribbing; circular 16" U.S. #8 (5mm) for neck ribbing

SIZES: XS (S, M, L)

KNITTED MEASUREMENTS: Width = 16$^1/_2$" (17$^1/_2$", 18$^1/_2$", 20"); Length = 22" (22$^1/_2$", 23$^1/_2$", 24"); Sleeve Length = 1/" (17$^1/_2$", 18, 18$^1/_2$")

Julie made a saddle shoulder turtleneck sweater for her husband, John, years ago. It had a tan body and brown sleeves and ribbing. She always loved the way it looked on him and always meant to make one for herself. But she had too many projects and never fit it in. Then, we started designing patterns for this book. We did a mental inventory of the sweaters we had made and helped our customers make, and Julie realized this was the perfect opportunity. It was now or never to make a pattern for a saddle shoulder of her own. We made one change to John's—instead of using two colors, we used one, but we knit in stockinette for the body and ribbed the sleeves.

BACK:

With #8 needle, cast on 58 (62, 66, 70) stitches. Work in K2, P2 ribbing for 6 rows as follows: ROW 1: K2, *P2, K2*. ROW 2: P2, *K2, P2*. Change to #10 needle and work in St st until piece measures 13$^1/_2$" (14", 14$^1/_2$", 14$^1/_2$") from the cast-on edge, ending with a WS row. SHAPE ARMHOLES: Bind off 3 stitches at the beginning of the next 2 rows. Bind off 2 stitches at the beginning of the following 2 rows. Then decrease 1 stitch at each edge, every other row 1 (2, 2, 3) time(s) until 46 (48, 52, 54) stitches remain. Continue work-ing in St st until piece measures 21" (21$^1/_2$", 22", 22$^1/_2$") from cast-on edge, ending with a WS row. SHAPE CREW NECK: Bind off 11 (12, 14, 14) stitches at the beginning of the next 2 rows. Continue in St st on remaining 24 (24, 24, 26) stitches until piece measures 22" (22$^1/_2$", 23$^1/_2$", 24") from cast-on edge, ending with a WS row. Bind off all stitches loosely.

FRONT:

With #8 needle, cast on 58 (62, 66, 70) stitches. Work in K2, P2 ribbing for 6 rows. Change to #10 needle and work in St st until piece measures 13$^1/_2$" (14", 14$^1/_2$", 14$^1/_2$") from the cast-on edge, ending with a WS row. SHAPE ARMHOLES: Bind off 3 stitches at the beginning of the next 2 rows. Bind off 2 stitches at the beginning of the following 2 rows. Then decrease 1 stitch at each edge, every other row 1 (2, 2, 3) time(s) until 46 (48, 52, 54) stitches remain. Continue working in St st until piece measures 19$^1/_2$" (20", 21", 21$^1/_2$") from cast-on edge, ending with a WS row. SHAPE CREW NECK: Bind off center 16 (16, 16, 18) stitches and then begin working each side of the neck separately. At the beginning of

each neck edge, every other row bind off 2 stitches 1 time, 1 stitch 2 times. Continue to work on remaining 11 (12, 14, 14) stitches with no further decreasing until piece measures 21" (21½", 22¼", 22½") from cast-on edge, ending with a WS row. Bind off all stitches loosely.

SLEEVES:

With #8 needle, cast on 32 (34, 36, 38) stitches. Work in K2, P2 ribbing as follows: For XS and M sizes: K2, P2 every row. For S and L sizes: **ROW 1:** K2 *P2, K2*. **ROW 2:** P2 *K2, P2*. **AT THE SAME TIME** increase in rib pattern one stitch at each edge, every 8th row 10 (10, 11, 12) times until you have 52 (54, 58, 62) stitches. *Note: Increase leaving 2 edge stitches on either side. This means you should work 2 stitches, increase a stitch, work to the last 2 stitches, increase a stitch, and then work the remaining 2 stitches. Increasing like this makes it easier to sew up your seams.* When sleeve measures 17" (17½", 18", 18½") from cast-on edge, ending with a WS row, S H A P E C A P: Bind off 3 stitches at the beginning of the next 2 rows. Bind off 2 stitches at the beginning of the following 2 rows. Then decrease 1 stitch at each edge, every other row 1 (2, 2, 3) time(s). Bind off 2 stitches at the beginning of the next 16 rows until 8 (8, 12, 14) stitches remain. Continue working in K2, P2 ribbing on remaining stitches until piece measures 3" (3½", 4", 4") from last bind off ending with a WS row. Bind off all stitches loosely.

FINISHING:

Sew shoulder seams together. Sew sleeves on. Then sew up side and sleeve seams.

With a circular 16" #8 needle, pick up 60 (60, 60, 64) stitches around neck and work in K2, P2 ribbing for 8". Bind off all stitches loosely.

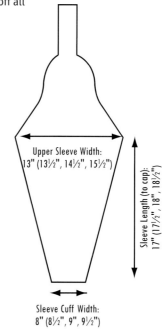

Upper Sleeve Width:
13" (13½", 14½", 15½")

Sleeve Length (to cap):
17" (17½", 18", 18½")

Sleeve Cuff Width:
8" (8½", 9", 9½")

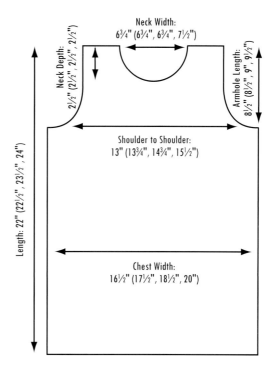

Neck Width:
6¾" (6¾", 6¾", 7½")

Neck Depth:
2½" (2½", 2½", 2½")

Armhole Length:
8½" (8½", 9", 9½")

Shoulder to Shoulder:
13" (13¾", 14¾", 15½")

Length: 22" (22½", 23½", 24")

Chest Width:
16½" (17½", 18½", 20")

a quick cowl

YARN: Crystal Palace Yarns, Merino Frappe (140 yards/50g ball)

FIBER CONTENT: 80% merino wool/20% polyamide

COLOR: 091

AMOUNT: 7 (7, 8, 9) balls

TOTAL YARDAGE: 980 (980, 1120, 1260) yards

GAUGE: 2½ stitches = 1 inch; 10 stitches = 4 inches

NEEDLE SIZE: U.S. #15 (10mm) for body or size needed to obtain gauge; circular 16" U.S. #13 (9mm) for neck ribbing

SIZES: XS (S, M, L)

KNITTED MEASUREMENTS: Width = 16" (17", 18½", 20"); Length = 21" (22", 23", 24"); Sleeve Length = 17½" (18", 18", 18½")

Yarn is worked double throughout the sweater—this means you should hold 2 strands of yarn together as if they were 1.

Dorothy is a busy woman. She's got an important job, three kids, and an addiction to knitting. When she comes into the store, she is all business. The last time Dorothy came in she wanted to make a sweater for her middle daughter, a woman in her mid-twenties who Dorothy describes as "stylish to a fault and very picky." She found this beautiful merino wool and decided that she wanted to make a cowl neck sweater. She began knitting a gauge so that we could write her a pattern. After a few minutes we began to hear some heavy sighs coming from her direction. "What's wrong?" we asked. "Well," she said "this is going to take me too long to knit. But I love the yarn—is there any way we can make it go faster?" "Of course," we responded. "We'll double the yarn, and then you can go on a nice big needle; it'll knit up in no time but will still feel light." Dorothy did her gauge, loved it, and promptly went home, knitting up the sweater in a matter of weeks.

BACK:

With #15 needle, cast on 40 (42, 46, 50) stitches. Work in St st until piece measures 13" (14", 14½", 15") from the cast-on edge, ending with a WS row. SHAPE ARMHOLES: Bind off 2 stitches at the beginning of the next 2 rows. Then decrease 1 stitch at each edge, every other row 2 (2, 3, 4) times until 32 (34, 36, 38) stitches remain. Continue working in St st until piece measures 21" (22", 23", 24") from cast-on edge, ending with a WS row. Bind off all stitches loosely.

FRONT:

With #15 needle, cast on 40 (42, 46, 50) stitches. Work in St st until piece measures 13" (14", 14½", 15") from the cast-on edge, ending with a WS row. SHAPE ARMHOLES: Bind off 2 stitches at the beginning of the next 2 rows. Then decrease 1 stitch at each edge, every other row 2 (2, 3, 4) times until 32 (34, 36, 38) stitches remain. Continue working in St st until piece measures 15" (16", 16", 16½") from cast-on edge, ending with a WS row. SHAPE CREW NECK: Bind off center 8 stitches and then begin working each side of the neck separately. At the beginning of each neck edge every other row, bind off 2 stitches 1 time, 1 stitch 2 (2, 2, 3) times. Continue to work on remaining 8 (9, 10, 10) stitches with no further decreasing until piece measures 21" (22", 23", 24") from cast-on edge, ending with a WS row. Bind off all stitches loosely.

SLEEVES:

With #15 needle, cast on 20 (22, 22, 24) stitches. Work in St st. **AT THE SAME TIME,** increase 1 stitch at each edge, every 8th row 5 (5, 6, 6) times until you have 30 (32, 34, 36) stitches. *Note: Increase leaving 2 edge stitches on either side of work. This means you should knit 2 stitches, increase a stitch, knit to the last 2 stitches, increase a stitch, and then knit the remaining 2 stitches. Increasing like this makes it easier to sew up your seams.* Continue in St st until sleeve measures 17½" (18", 18", 18½") from cast-on edge, ending with a WS row. SHAPE CAP: Bind off 2 stitches at the beginning of the next 2 rows. Then decrease 1 stitch at each edge, every other row 2 (2, 3, 4) times. Bind off 2 stitches at the beginning of the next 8 rows. Bind off remaining 6 (8, 8, 8) stitches loosely.

FINISHING:

Sew shoulder seams together. Sew sleeves on. Then sew up side and sleeve seams.

With a circular 16" #13 needle, pick up 88 (88, 88, 90) stitches around neck. Work in K1, P1 ribbing for 8". Bind off all stitches loosely.

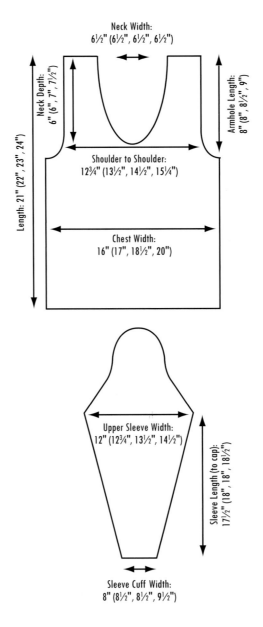

Neck Width: 6½" (6½", 6½", 6½")

Neck Depth: 6" (6", 7", 7½")

Armhole Length: 8" (8", 8½", 9")

Length: 21" (22", 23", 24")

Shoulder to Shoulder: 12¾" (13½", 14½", 15¼")

Chest Width: 16" (17", 18½", 20")

Upper Sleeve Width: 12" (12¾", 13½", 14½")

Sleeve Length (to cap): 17½" (18", 18", 18½")

Sleeve Cuff Width: 8" (8½", 8½", 9½")

for a good cause

YARN: S. Charles, Ritratto (198 yards/ 50g ball)

FIBER CONTENT: 30% mohair/50% viscose/10% polyamide/10% polyester

COLOR: 63

AMOUNT: 3 (3, 4, 4) balls

TOTAL YARDAGE: 594 (594, 792, 792) yards

GAUGE: 5¾ stitches = 1 inch; 23 stitches = 4 inches

NEEDLE SIZE: U.S. #6 (4mm) or size needed to obtain gauge; G crochet hook

SIZES: XS (S, M, L)

With all the recent hurricanes and natural disasters, there have been a lot of fundraiser auctions. Beryl donated her time to knit a sweater to auction off. Since the holidays were coming up, we decided the sweater should be simply styled, festive, and perfect for parties. We chose a yarn with shimmer and texture and designed a sexy tank top with a crochet edging. The highest bidder just loves it!

BACK:

With #6 needle, cast on 92 (98, 104, 110) stitches. Work in St st until piece measures 13½" (14", 14½", 15") from the cast-on edge, ending with a WS row. SHAPE ARMHOLES: Bind off 5 stitches at the beginning of the next 2 rows. Bind off 3 stitches at the beginning of the following 2 rows. Bind off 2 stitches at the beginning of the next 2 rows. Then decrease 1 stitch at each edge, every other row 3 (3, 4, 5) times until 66 (72, 76, 80) stitches remain. Continue working in St st until piece measures 20" (21", 22", 23") from cast-on edge, ending with a WS row. Bind off all stitches loosely.

FRONT:

Work as for Back until piece measures 13½" (14", 14½", 15") from the cast-on edge, ending with a WS row. SHAPE ARMHOLES: Bind off 5 stitches at the beginning of the next 2 rows. Bind off 3 stitches at the beginning of the following 2 rows. Bind off 2 stitches at the beginning of the next 2 rows. Then decrease 1 stitch at each edge, every other row 3 (3, 4, 5) times until 66 (72, 76, 80) stitches remain. Continue working in St st until piece measures 17½" (18½", 19½", 20½") from cast-on edge, ending with a WS row. SHAPE CREW NECK: Bind off center 20 (20, 22, 24) stitches and then begin working each side of the neck separately. At the beginning of each neck edge, every other row bind off 3 stitches 1 time, 2 stitches 1 time, and 1 stitch 4 times. Continue to work on remaining 14 (17, 18, 19) stitches with no further decreasing until piece measures 20" (21", 22", 23") from cast-on edge, ending with a WS row. Bind off all stitches loosely.

FINISHING:

Sew shoulder seams together. Sew side seams down. With G crochet hook, work 1 row of single crochet and 1 row of shrimp stitch around all edges.

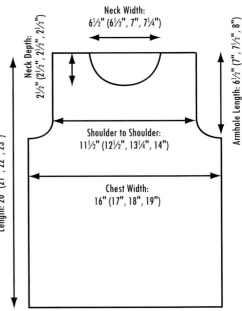

Neck Width: 6½" (6½", 7", 7¼")

Neck Depth: 2½" (2½", 2½", 2½")

Armhole Length: 6½" (7", 7½", 8")

Shoulder to Shoulder: 11½" (12½", 13¼", 14")

Length: 20" (21", 22", 23")

Chest Width: 16" (17", 18", 19")

knitting in the dark

YARN: A: Karabella, Aurora Bulky (56 yards /50g ball); B: Karabella Fur

FIBER CONTENT: A: 100% merino wool; B: 100% rabbit fur

COLORS: A: 3; B: 4

AMOUNT: A: 13 (14, 15, 16) balls; B: 6 (6, 7, 7) yards

TOTAL YARDAGE: A: 728 (784, 840, 896); B: 6 (6, 7, 7) yards

GAUGE: $3^1/_2$ stitches = 1 inch; 14 stitches = 4 inches

NEEDLE SIZE: U.S. #$10^1/_2$ (7mm) or size needed to obtain gauge; I (5.5mm) crochet hook

SIZES: XS (S, M, L)

KNITTED MEASUREMENTS: Width = 17" ($17^1/_2$", $18^1/_2$", 20"); Length = $19^1/_2$" ($20^1/_2$", 22", 24"); Sleeve Length = 17" ($17^1/_2$", 18", $18^1/_2$")

Julie's two-year-old daughter, Olivia, had been sick. Usually a good sleeper, Olivia woke up at 2:00 a.m. for a week. The only way Julie could get her back to sleep was by sleeping with her on the couch. Olivia hogged the couch and snored terribly (due to her stuffy nose), so Julie just sat on the edge of the couch, miserable. On the second night, Julie started to flip through a magazine. It was hard to see in the dark, but she could make out the photographs and noticed a cute Chanel-type jacket that the model was wearing with jeans. Julie decided she needed one, but she knew she would have little time to shop. The next night, Olivia still sick and snoring, Julie pulled out a few balls of yarn and decided to make good use of her sleeplessness to knit the jacket. She knit it in a two-row pattern for added texture and decided that when it was done, she would trim it with fur. By the time Olivia was better, Julie was almost done with the sweater. She was also very tired.

PATTERN STITCH:

Over even number of stitches:
ROW 1 AND 2: K1, P1.
ROW 3 AND 4: P1, K1.
Over odd number of stitches:
ROW 1 AND 4: K1 *(P1, K1)*.
ROW 2 AND 3: P1 *(K1, P1) *.

BACK:

With #$10^1/_2$ needle and **color A,** cast on 60 (62, 66, 70) stitches. Work in pattern stitch until piece measures $11^1/_2$" (12", $13^1/_4$", 15") from cast-on edge, ending with a WS row. SHAPE ARM-HOLES: Bind off 3 stitches at the beginning of the next 2 rows. Bind off 2 stitches at the beginning of the next two rows. Then decrease 1 stitch at each edge, every other row 1 (1, 2, 2) time(s) until 48 (50, 52, 56) stitches remain. Continue to work in pattern stitch until piece measures $19^1/_2$" ($20^1/_2$", 22", 24") from cast-on edge, ending with a WS row. Bind off all stitches loosely.

FRONT: (MAKE 2, REVERSE SHAPING)

With #10½ needle and **color A,** cast on 30 (31, 33, 35) stitches. Work in pattern stitch until piece measures 11½" (12", 13¼", 15") from cast-on edge, ending with a WS row for the left front and a RS row for the right front. SHAPE ARM-HOLES AS FOR BACK AT SIDE EDGE ONLY until 24 (25, 26, 28) stitches remain. Continue to work in pattern stitch until piece measures 17" (18", 19½", 21½") from cast-on edge, ending with a RS row for the left front and a WS row for the right front. SHAPE CREW NECK: At beginning of neck edge, every other row bind off 4 stitches 1 time, 3 stitches 1 time, 2 stitches 1 time, and 1 stitch 1 (1, 2, 2) time(s). Continue to work in St st on remaining 14 (15, 15, 17) stitches in pattern stitch until piece measures 19½" (20½", 22", 24") from cast-on edge ending with a WS row. Bind off all stitches loosely.

SLEEVES:

With #10½ needle and **color A,** cast on 28 (30, 32, 32) stitches. Work in pattern stitch. **AT THE SAME TIME,** increase 1 stitch at each edge, every 8th row 10 (10, 10, 11) times until you have 48 (50, 52, 54) stitches. *Note: Increase leaving 2 edge stitches on either side. This means you should work 2 stitches, increase a stitch, work to the last 2 stitches, increase a stitch, and then work the remaining 2 stitches. Increasing like this makes it easier to sew up your seams.* When sleeve measures 17" (17½", 18", 18½") from cast-on edge, ending with a WS row, SHAPE CAP: Bind off 3 stitches at the beginning of the next 2 rows. Bind off 2 stitches at the beginning of the next 2 rows. Then decrease 1 stitch at each edge, every other row 1 (1, 2, 2) time(s). Bind off 2 stitches at the begin-

ning of the next 12 rows until 12 (14, 14, 16) stitches remain. Bind off all stitches loosely.

FINISHING:

Sew shoulder seams together. Sew sleeves on. Sew up side and sleeve seams. With an I crochet hook, work 1 row single crochet, and 1 row shrimp stitch around all edges. With **color B** and a large-eyed sewing needle, whipstitch around all edges. Insert needle every 1½".

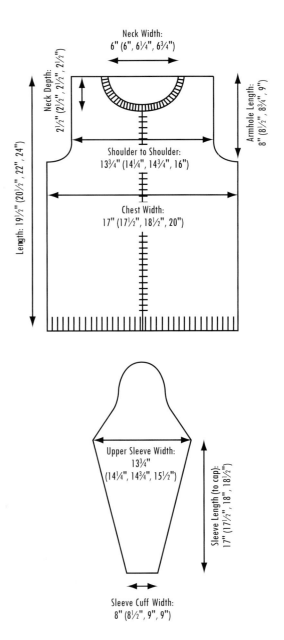

Neck Width:
6" (6", 6¼", 6¾")

Neck Depth:
2½" (2½", 2½", 2½")

Armhole Length:
8" (8½", 8¾", 9")

Length: 19½" (20½", 22", 24")

Shoulder to Shoulder:
13¾" (14¼", 14¾", 16")

Chest Width:
17" (17½", 18½", 20")

Upper Sleeve Width:
13¾"
(14¼", 14¾", 15½")

Sleeve Length (to cap):
17" (17½", 18", 18½")

Sleeve Cuff Width:
8" (8½", 9", 9")

credit where credit is due

YARN: A: GGH, Savanna (84 yards/50g ball); B: S. Charles Ritratto (198 yards/50g ball)

FIBER CONTENT: A: 43% alpaca/23% linen/19% wool/15% nylon; B: 28% mohair/53% viscose/10% polyamide/9% polyester

COLORS: A: 7; B: 81

AMOUNT: A: 6 (6, 7, 8); B: 3 (3, 3, 4) balls

TOTAL YARDAGE: A: 504 (504, 588, 672); B: 594 (594, 594, 792) yards

GAUGE: 3 stitches = 1 inch; 12 stitches = 4 inches

NEEDLE SIZE: U.S. #11 (8mm) or size needed to obtain gauge; U.S. #10 (6mm) for ribbing

SIZES: XS (S, M, L)

OTHER MATERIALS: Elastic

Yarn is worked double throughout the skirt—this means you should hold 1 strand of A and 1 strand of B together as if they were 1.

Evelyn has a great sense of style. She is a very creative knitter and loves to knit suits and skirts. One day, she came to the store with a picture of a chunky skirt that had a bit of a flounce on its bottom and told us this is what she wanted to make. She then proceeded to walk around the store, picking up yarns. Eventually, Evelyn sat down at the table that is in the middle of our store with two yarns and told us that these were the yarns she wanted to use for the skirt. We looked at Evelyn, then at each other, and shrugged—she'd combined yarns we wouldn't have thought to put together, but if that's what she wanted to make a skirt out of, then who were we to argue. The skirt is knit in the round from the bottom up and uses simple decreasing to create the flared bottom. A week or two later, Evelyn walked in wearing our creation—it looked great on her. We asked her if she would mind if we put the design in our new book, and she said she'd love it—as long as we gave her some of the credit.

SKIRT:

With #11 circular needle and 1 strand of **color A** and 1 strand of **color B,** cast on 189 (196, 203, 210) stitches. Place a marker at the beginning of your row and join stitches in a circle. Make sure that all stitches are facing the same way and that you are not twisting them. Work 1 row in K1, P1 ribbing, then continue in St st for 6 rounds.

Place markers:

FOR XS: *pm, K 10 stitches, pm, K 17 stitches* repeat around.

FOR S: *pm, K 11 stitches, pm, K 17 stitches* repeat around.

FOR M: *pm, K 11 stitches, pm, K 18 stitches* repeat around.

FOR L: *pm, K 12 stitches, pm, K 18 stitches* repeat around.

NEXT ROUND (DECREASE ROW): Work decreases at either end of the 17th/18th stitches as follows:

Slip 1 stitch knitwise, K1, psso, knit until 2 stitches before marker, K2tog.

Repeat this decrease row, every 6th round 6 more times. You will be decreasing 14 stitches each time you decrease. Remove all markers except for the one that marks the beginning of the row. You will now have 91 (98, 105, 112) stitches. For XS and M: K2tog at the beginning of the next round. You will now have 90 (98, 104, 112) stitches.

Continue in St st with no further decreasing until piece measures 22" (24", 26", 28").

NEXT ROUND: Knit until 6 stitches before marker, pm, K12, pm, K33 (37, 40, 44), pm, K12, pm, K33 (37, 40, 44), knit to marker, slip marker.

NEXT ROUND: K2tog, K8, sl1, K1, psso, slip marker, knit to next marker, slip marker and repeat. Knit to end of round.

NEXT ROUND: K2tog, K6, sl1, K1, psso, slip marker, knit to next marker, slip marker and repeat. Knit to end of round.

NEXT ROUND: K2tog, K4, sl1, K1, psso, slip

marker, knit to next marker, slip marker and repeat. Knit to end of round.

NEXT ROUND: K2tog, K2, sl1, K1, psso, slip marker, knit to next marker, slip marker and repeat. Knit to end of round.

NEXT ROUND: K2tog, sl1, K1, psso, slip marker, knit to next marker, slip marker and repeat. Knit to end of round.

You will now have 70 (78, 84, 92) stitches. Change to #10 needles and continue in K1, P1 ribbing until the ribbing measures 4". Bind off all stitches loosely.

FINISHING:

Fold ribbing in half, place elastic inside, and stitch down.

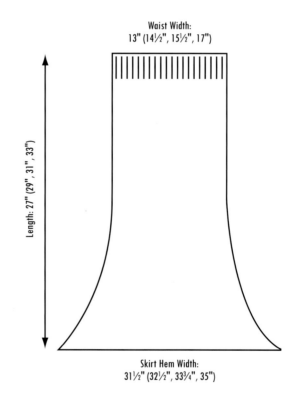

Waist Width:
13" (14½", 15½", 17")

Length: 27" (29", 31", 33")

Skirt Hem Width:
31½" (32½", 33¾", 35")

out of retirement

YARN: Filatura di Crosa, Cashmere
(156 yards/50g ball)

FIBER CONTENT: 100% cashmere

COLOR: 400003

AMOUNT: 2 balls

TOTAL YARDAGE: 312 yards

GAUGE: 3¼ stitches = 1 inch; 13 stitches
= 4 inches

NEEDLE SIZE: U.S. #10 (6mm) or size
needed to obtain gauge

SIZES: XS (S, M, L)

KNITTED MEASUREMENTS:
circumference = 18" (19", 20", 21½")

OTHER MATERIALS: One button

*Yarn is worked double throughout
the hat—this means you should hold
2 strands of yarn together as if they
were 1.*

Julien recently bought a great winter coat. It was slim-fitting, with a slightly vintage look. After buying the coat, she decided that she also needed the perfect winter hat. However, after searching store after store, she could not find exactly what she had envisioned. Julien decided that the only way she was going to get what she wanted was to design and make it herself. Having retired her needles for a good number of years, Julien found that it was time to start knitting again. She came into the store and drew us a picture of exactly what she wanted. It was a simple shape, with a garter band on the bottom and seed stitch on the top. She also wanted a little button on the side of the hat. We envisioned this cloche in cashmere, the ultimate luxury in hand knits, but a soft merino wool will do the job equally well. We wrote her the pattern, and it came out exactly as she'd hoped. She vowed never to put her needles down again.

HAT:

With #10 needle and 2 strands of yarn, cast on 64 (68, 72, 76) stitches. Work in garter stitch for 2 rows. Make buttonhole: K3, YO, K2tog, knit to end of row. Continue in garter stitch for 3 more rows. **NEXT ROW:** Bind off 6 stitches, knit to end. You now have 58 (62, 66, 70) stitches. **NEXT ROW:** Begin to work in seed stitch as follows: **ROW 1:** K1, P1. **ROW 2:** P1, K1. Work in seed stitch until piece measures 5" (5½", 6", 6½"), ending with a row 2.
Decrease as follows:

For XS:
ROW 1: *(K1, P1) twice, K1, P3tog* repeat from * to * across row, end (K1, P1). (44 stitches)
ROW 2: P1, K1 across row.
ROW 3: *(K1, P1) twice, K3tog, (P1, K1) twice, P3tog* repeat from * to * across row, end K1, P1. (32 stitches)

ROW 4: P1, K1 across row.

ROW 5: *K1, P1, K1, P3tog* repeat from * to * across row, end K1, P1. (22 stitches)

ROW 6: P1, K1 across row.

ROW 7: *(K1, P1, K3tog, P1, K1, P3 tog) twice*, end K1, P1. (14 stitches)

ROW 8: P1, K1 across row.

ROW 9: *K1, P3tog* across row, end K1, P1. (8 stitches)

ROW 10: P1, K1 across row.

For S:

ROW 1: *(K1 P1) twice, K1, P3tog* repeat from * to * across row, end (K1, P1) 3 times. (48 stitches)

ROW 2: P1, K1 across row.

ROW 3: *(K1, P1) twice, K3tog, (P1, K1) twice, P3tog* repeat from * to * across row, end (K1, P1) 3 times. (36 stitches).

ROW 4: P1, K1 across row.

ROW 5: *K1, P1, K1, P3tog* repeat from * to * across row. (24 stitches)

ROW 6: P1, K1 across row.

ROW 7: *K1, P1, K3tog, P1, K1, P3 tog*, end (K1, P1) twice. (16 stitches)

ROW 8: P1, K1 across row.

ROW 9: *K1, P3tog* across row. (8 stitches)

ROW 10: P1, K1 across row.

For M:

ROW 1: *(K1 P1) twice, K1, P3tog* repeat from * to * across row, end, (K1, P1). (50 stitches)

ROW 2: P1, K1 across row.

ROW 3: *(K1, P1) twice, K3tog, (P1, K1) twice, P3tog* repeat from * to * across row, end (K1, P1) twice, K3tog, P1. (36 stitches)

ROW 4: P1, K1 across row.

ROW 5: *K1, P1, K1, P3tog* repeat from *

to * across row. (24 stitches)

ROW 6: P1, K1 across row.

ROW 7: *K1, P1, K3tog, P1, K1, P3 tog*, end (K1, P1) twice. (16 stitches)

ROW 8: P1, K1 across row.

ROW 9: *K1, P3tog* across row. (8 stitches)

ROW 10: P1, K1 across row.

For L:

ROW 1: *(K1 P1) twice, K1, P3tog* repeat from * to * across row, end (K1, P1) 3 times. (54 stitches)

ROW 2: P1, K1 across row.

ROW 3: *(K1, P1) twice, K3tog, (P1, K1) twice, P3tog* repeat from * to * across row, end (K1, P1) twice, K3tog, P1, K1, P1. (40 stitches)

ROW 4: P1, K1 across row.

ROW 5: *K1, P1, K1, P3tog* repeat from * to * across row, end (K1, P1) twice. (28 stitches)

ROW 6: P1, K1 across row.

ROW 7: *K1, P1, K3tog, P1, K1, P3tog*, repeat from * to * across row, end K1, P1, K3tog, P1, K1, P1. (18 stitches)

ROW 8: P1, K1 across row.

ROW 9: *K1, P3tog* repeat from * to * across row, end K1, P1. (10 stitches)

ROW 10: P1, K1 across row.

FINISHING:

Cut yarn, leaving 12". Thread on a sewing needle and pull through remaining stitches. Sew up seam and attach button.

becoming the bag lady

YARN: Blue Sky Alpacas, Alpaca Worsted (100 yards/100g ball)

FIBER CONTENT: 50% alpaca/50% merino wool

COLOR: 2002

AMOUNT: 2 balls

TOTAL YARDAGE: 200 yards

GAUGE: 4 stitches = 1 inch; 16 stitches = 4 inches

NEEDLE SIZE: U.S. #10 (6mm) or size needed to obtain gauge; U.S. #8 (5mm) circular or double-pointed for I-cord; K (6.5mm) crochet hook

SIZES: One size

OTHER MATERIALS: One button

Jennifer was looking to knit something fresh and atypical. She was a voracious knitter who had knit many sweaters, hats, ponchos, scarves, and blankets. But she'd come to a point in her knitting career where she felt like she had done it all. She wanted a truly new project. While she was searching for her project at our store, another customer walked in wearing a beautiful designer knit bag. A light went off in Jennifer's head: That was it—a bag! Jennifer got excited—she'd never knit a bag before. Later that week she came in with a few design ideas, and we worked out this cabled pattern for her. Jennifer loved her bag so much that bags became her new obsession. What will she make when she tires of them?

SPECIAL STITCHES:

C2B (Cable 2 into back): Slip 1 stitch to cable needle, hold at back, knit 1 stitch from left-hand needle, knit 1 from cable needle.

C2F (Cable 2 into front): Slip 1 stitch to cable needle, hold at front, knit 1 stitch from left-hand needle, knit 1 from cable needle.

C3B (Cable 3 into back): Slip 2 stitches onto cable needle, hold at back, knit 1 stitch from left-hand needle, knit 2 stitches from cable needle.

C3F (Cable 3 into front): Slip 1 stitch onto cable needle, hold at front, knit 2 stitches from left-hand needle, knit 1 stitch from cable needle.

C6B (Cable 6 into back): Slip 3 stitches to cable needle, hold at back, knit 3

stitches from left-hand needle, knit 3 stitches from cable needle.

CABLE PATTERN:

ROW 1: P4, C2F, C2B, P2, K6, P2, C2B, P2, K6, P2, C2B, P2, K6, P2, C2F, C2B, P4.

ROW 2: K4, P4, K2, P6, K2, P2, K2, P6, K2, P2, K2, P6, K2, P4, K4.

ROW 3: P4, K4, P2, K6, P2, C2B, P2, C3B,

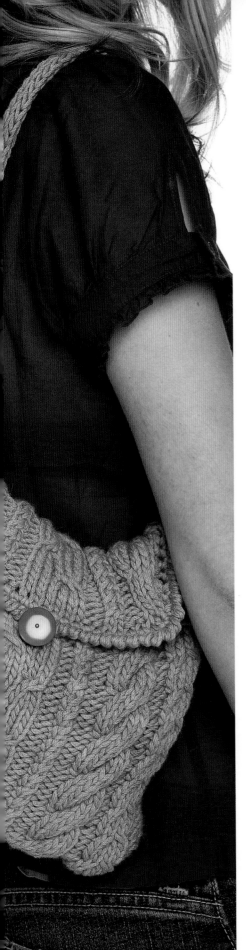

K3, P2, C2B, P2, K6, P2, K4, P4.

ROW 4: Same as row 2.

ROW 5: P4, C2F, C2B, P2, C6B, P2, C2B, P2, K6, P2, C2B, P2, C6B, P2, C2F, C2B, P4.

ROW 6: Same as row 2.

ROW 7: P4, K4, P2, K6, P2, C2B, P2, K3, C3F, P2, C2B, P2, K6, P2, K4, P4.

ROW 8: Same as row 2.

ROW 9: P4, C2F, C2B, P2, K6, P2, C2B, P2, K6, P2, C2B, P2, K6, P2, C2F, C2B, P4.

ROW 10: Same as row 2.

ROW 11: P4, K4, P2, C6B, P2, C2B, P2, C3B, K3, P2, C2B, P2, C6B, P2, K4, P4.

ROW 12: Same as row 2.

ROW 13: P4, C2F, C2B, P2, K6, P2, C2B, P2, K6, P2, C2B, P2, K6, P2, C2F, C2B, P4.

ROW 14: Same as row 2.

ROW 15: P4, K4, P2, K6, P2, C2B, P2, K3, C3F, P2, C2B, P2, K6, P2, K4, P4.

ROW 16: Same as row 2.

ROW 17: P4, C2F, C2B, P2, C6B, P2, C2B, P2, K6, P2, C2B, P2, C6B, P2, C2F, C2B, P4.

ROW 18: Same as row 2.

ROW 19: P4, K4, P2, K6, P2, C2B, P2, C3B, K3, P2, C2B, P2, K6, P2, K4, P4.

ROW 20: Same as row 2.

ROW 21: P4, C2F, C2B, P2, K6, P2, C2B, P2, K6, P2, C2B, P2, K6, P2, C2F, C2B, P4.

ROW 22: Same as row 2.

ROW 23: P4, K4, P2, C6B, P2, C2B, P2, K3, C3F, P2, C2B, P2, C6B, P2, K4, P4.

ROW 24: Same as row 2.

Repeat rows 1–24 to form pattern.

FRONT:

With #10 needle, cast on 50 stitches. Work in cable pattern until piece measures 6¹/₂" from cast-on edge, ending with a WS row. Bind off 4 stitches at the beginning of the next 2 rows. You will now have 42 stitches. Continue in cable pattern (without the P4/K4 on either end) until piece measures 8" from cast-on edge, ending with a WS row. Bind off all stitches loosely.

BACK:

With #10 needle, cast on 50 stitches. Work in cable pattern as for back until piece measures 6¹/₂" from cast-on edge, ending with a WS row. Bind off 4 stitches at the beginning of the next 2 rows. You will now have 42 stitches. Continue in cable pattern (without the P4/K4 on either end) until piece measures 8¹/₂" from cast-on edge, ending with a WS row. Then bind off 2 stitches at the beginning of the next 10 rows. Bind off the remaining 22 stitches loosely.

HANDLE:

With #8 needle, cast on 5 stitches. Make an I-cord that is 22" long.

FINISHING:

Sew sides and bottom together. Attach I-cord to sides of bag. With K crochet hook, work 1 row single crochet and 1 row shrimp stitch, making a button loop in center around front flap. Sew on button.

three out of four knitters recommend this sweater

YARN: Lang, Naima (65 yards/50g ball)

FIBER CONTENT: 50% alpaca/50% merino wool

COLOR: 68

AMOUNT: 13 (14, 15, 16) balls

TOTAL YARDAGE: 845 (910, 975, 1040) yards

GAUGE: 3 stitches = 1 inch; 12 stitches = 4 inches

NEEDLE SIZE: U.S. #11 (8mm) or size needed to obtain gauge; circular 16" U.S. #11 (8mm) for ribbing

SIZES: S (M, L, XL)

KNITTED MEASUREMENTS: Width = 22" (23$\frac{1}{2}$", 25", 25$\frac{1}{2}$"); Length = 23" (24", 25", 26"); Sleeve Length = 18" (19", 19$\frac{1}{2}$", 20")

One day Bill and a few women were sitting at our knitting table comparing projects they were working on. Bill was knitting himself a basic crew neck pullover sweater that we had designed, and all the women were so impressed and loved it. It was a seeded rib sweater knit from a tweedy yarn—a great pattern for knitters who are getting a little tired of basic stockinette stitch but don't want to commit to anything too complicated. This sweater is one of those pieces that could be worn all weekend long. Three out of four of the women sitting in our shop quickly decided to knit the same one for the men in their lives. Hopefully, four out of four of you will feel the same way.

PATTERN STITCH:
(FOR BACK AND FRONT ONLY)

For sizes S and XL:
ROW 1: K6 *Seed 5, K5* end K1.
ROW 2: P6 *Seed 5, P5* end P1.

For size M:
ROW 1: K3 *Seed 5, K5* end Seed 5, K3.
ROW 2: P3 *Seed 5, P5* end Seed 5, P3.
For size L:
ROW 1: K5 *Seed 5, K5*.
ROW 2: P5 *Seed 5, P5*.

BACK:

With #11 needle, cast on 67 (71, 75, 77) stitches. Work in pattern until piece measures 14" (14$\frac{1}{2}$", 15", 15$\frac{1}{2}$") from the cast-on edge, ending with a WS row.
SHAPE ARMHOLES: Bind off 3 stitches at the beginning of the next 2

rows. Bind off 2 stitches at the beginning of the following 2 rows. Then decrease 1 stitch at each edge, every other row 3 (4, 4, 3) times until 51 (53, 57, 61) stitches remain. Continue working in pattern stitch until piece measures 23" (24", 25", 26") from cast-on edge, ending with a WS row. Bind off all stitches loosely.

FRONT:

With #11 needle, cast on 67 (71, 75, 77) stitches. Work in pattern until piece measures 14" (14½", 15", 15½") from the cast-on edge, ending with a WS row. SHAPE ARMHOLES: Bind off 3 stitches at the beginning of the next 2 rows. Bind off 2 stitches at the beginning of the following 2 rows. Then decrease 1 stitch at each edge, every other row 3 (4, 4, 3) times until 51 (53, 57, 61) stitches remain. Continue working in pattern stitch until piece measures 20½" (21½", 22½", 23½") from cast-on edge, ending with a WS row. SHAPE CREW NECK: Bind off center 13 stitches and

then begin working each side of the neck separately. At the beginning of each neck edge, every other row bind off 2 stitches 1 time, 1 stitch 3 times. Continue to work on remaining 14 (15, 17, 19) stitches with no further decreasing until piece measures 23" (24", 25", 26") from cast-on edge, ending with a WS row. Bind off all stitches loosely.

SLEEVES:

With #11 needle, cast on 26 (28, 30, 30) stitches. Work in pattern stitch as follows: For sizes L and XL: ROW 1: *K5, Seed 5*. ROW 2: *Seed 5, P5*. For size S: ROW 1: Seed 3 * K5, Seed 5*, end K3. ROW 2: P3 *Seed 5, P5* end P3. For size M: ROW 1: Seed 4 * K5, Seed 5*, end K4. ROW 2: P4 *Seed 5, P5*, end P4. **AT THE SAME TIME,** increase 1 stitch in pattern at each edge, every 6th row 11 (11, 11, 12) times until you have 48 (50, 52, 54) stitches. *Note: Increase leaving 2 edge stitches on either side. This means you should work 2 stitches, increase a stitch,*

work to the last 2 stitches, increase a stitch, and then work the remaining 2 stitches. Increasing like this makes it easier to sew up your seams. When sleeve measures 18" (19", 19½", 20") from cast-on edge, ending with a WS row, SHAPE CAP: Bind off 3 stitches at the beginning of the next 2 rows. Bind off 2 stitches at the beginning of the following 2 rows. Then decrease 1 stitch at each edge, every other row 3 (4, 4, 3) times. Bind off 2 stitches at the beginning of the next 10 (10, 12, 12) rows until 12 (12, 10, 14) stitches remain. Bind off all stitches loosely.

FINISHING:

Sew shoulder seams together. Sew sleeves on. Then sew up side and sleeve seams.

With a circular 16" #11 needle, pick up 60 stitches around neck and work in Seed 5, K5 ribbing for 6 rows. Bind off all stitches loosely.

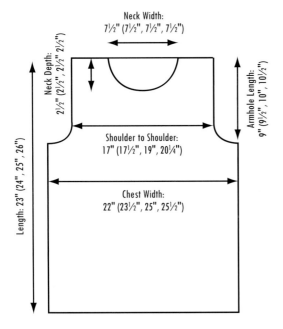

Neck Width:
7½" (7½", 7½", 7½")

Neck Depth:
2½" (2½", 2½" 2½")

Armhole Length:
9" (9½", 10", 10½")

Length: 23" (24", 25", 26")

Shoulder to Shoulder:
17" (17½", 19", 20¼")

Chest Width:
22" (23½", 25", 25½")

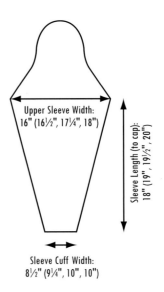

Upper Sleeve Width:
16" (16½", 17¼", 18")

Sleeve Length (to cap):
18" (19", 19½", 20")

Sleeve Cuff Width:
8½" (9¼", 10", 10")

it's the thought that Counts

YARN: Rowan, Biggy Print (33 yards/100g ball)

FIBER CONTENT: 100% merino wool

COLOR: 252

AMOUNT: 15 (16, 18, 20) balls

TOTAL YARDAGE: 495 (528, 594, 660) yards

GAUGE: $1^7/_{10}$ stitches = 1 inch; 7 stitches = 4 inches; $2^1/_2$ rows = 1 inch; 10 rows = 4 inches

NEEDLE SIZE: U.S. #17 (12 mm) for body or size needed to obtain gauge; U.S. #15 (10 mm) for ribbing; circular 17" U.S. #17 (12mm) for neck ribbing

SIZES: S (M, L XL)

KNITTED MEASUREMENTS: Width = 22" (23", 24", $25^1/_2$"); Length = 24" (25", 26", 27"); Sleeve Length = 18" ($18^1/_2$", 20", 21")

Shannon was a prolific knitter, but he had never knit for himself. He knit on the subway, in the movies, on his couch, and even at meetings during work. After watching his needles click away, everyone at work wanted to learn to knit. So Shannon organized a few Sunday morning brunches, and he began teaching his coworkers. He was so patient and giving of his time that his coworkers wanted to do something nice for him. After much debate and a bit of practice, they decided to make Shannon a sweater. They came to us and asked for our advice. We thought it should be a quickly knit sweater that Shannon could wear to keep warm in the middle of winter. So we designed a simple raglan turtleneck. The texture of this yarn varies from thick to thin, and it knits up super fast for a sweater that you can make in a matter of days. Each coworker knit a piece. Their gauges were not all exactly the same, but it's the thought that counts. The sweater turned out great, and Shannon was so appreciative.

BACK AND FRONT:

With #15 needle, cast on 40 (42, 44, 46) stitches. Work in K2, P2 rib for 4 rows as follows: For sizes S and L: K2, P2 every row. For M and XL: **ROW 1:** K2 *P2, K2.* **ROW 2:** P2 *K2, P2*. Change to #17 needle and work in St st until piece measures 14" (14", 14", 14½") from cast-on edge, ending with a WS row. S H A P E R A G L A N A R M H O L E S: Bind off 2 stitches at the beginning of the next 2 rows. Then work **ROW 1:** K2, SSK, pattern to end. **ROW 2:** P2, P2tog, pattern to end. Repeat rows 1 and 2 11 (12, 13, 14) more times until 12 stitches remain. Bind off all stitches loosely.

SLEEVES:

With #15 needle, cast on 20 (20, 22, 22) stitches. Work in K2, P2 rib for 4 rows as follows: For sizes S and M: K2, P2 every row. For L and XL: **ROW 1:** K2 *P2, K2.* **ROW 2:** P2 *K2, P2.* Change to #17 needle and work in St st. **AT THE SAME TIME,** increase 1 stitch at each edge, every 6th row 5 (4, 5, 4) times, every 4th row 1 (3, 2, 4) time(s) until you have 32

(34, 36, 38) stitches. *Note: Increase leaving 2 edge stitches on either side of work. This means you should knit 2 stitches, increase a stitch, knit to the last 2 stitches, increase a stitch, and then knit the remaining 2 stitches. Increasing like this makes it easier to sew up your seams.* Continue in St st until sleeve measures 18" (18½", 19½", 20") from cast-on edge, ending with a WS row. S H A P E R A G L A N S L E E V E: Bind off 2 stitches at the beginning of the next 2 rows. Then work **ROW 1:** K2, SSK, pattern to end. **ROW 2:** P2, P2tog, pattern to end. Repeat rows 1 and 2 11 (12, 13, 14) times until 4 stitches remain. Bind off all stitches loosely.

FINISHING:

Sew raglan pieces together. With #17 16" circular needle and right side facing, pick up 12 stitches along back neck, 4 stitches along left sleeve, 12 stitches along front neck, and 4 stitches along right sleeve. Work in K2, P2 ribbing for 7". Bind off all stitches loosely.

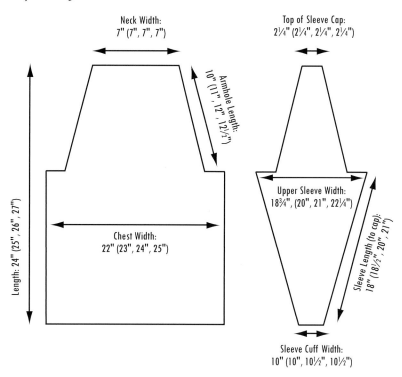

Neck Width:
7" (7", 7", 7")

Top of Sleeve Cap:
2¼" (2¼", 2¼", 2¼")

Armhole Length:
10" (11", 12", 12½")

Length: 24" (25", 26", 27")

Chest Width:
22" (23", 24", 25")

Upper Sleeve Width:
18¾", (20", 21", 22¼")

Sleeve Length (to cap):
18" (18½", 20", 21")

Sleeve Cuff Width:
10" (10", 10½", 10½")

FINISHING TECHNIQUES

You can spend hours knitting row after row of perfect ribbing and flawless stockinette stitch, but all those efforts can be undermined by sloppy finishing technique. Knowing how to sew a sweater together properly is the ultimate key to whether the sweater looks handmade— or homemade. If you use the proper techniques, the process should be relatively painless and your sweater should look virtually seamless. And a final steaming, known as blocking, will smooth over any inconsistencies or bumpy seams.

Some tips:

- Sweaters are always sewn on the right side.

- Although other people might tell you differently, we prefer **not** to use the yarn we knit our sweater with to sew it together. Generally, we suggest using a needlepoint yarn in a similar color, because using a different yarn allows you to see what you are doing much more clearly. And, dare we say it, it also enables you to rip out what you have done, if necessary, without inadvertently damaging the sweater itself.

Whether you are making a V-neck, a turtleneck, a crew neck, or a cardigan, sweaters are always assembled in the same order:

1. Sew shoulder seams together.

2. Sew sleeves onto sweater.

3. Sew sleeve seams from armhole to cuff.

4. Sew side seams from armhole to waist.

Once the pieces are joined together, you can add crochet edgings, pick up stitches for a neck, create button bands for a cardigan, or embellish your project with other finishing touches.

sewing shoulder seams

1. Lay the front and back of your sweater flat with the right sides facing you and the shoulders pointing toward each other. If you are sewing the shoulder seams of a cardigan together, make sure the armholes are facing away from the center and the neck toward the center. (Illus. A)

2. Cut a piece of sewing yarn approximately twice the width of your shoulder seam and thread it through a darning needle.

3. Secure the sewing yarn to the garment by making a knot with one end of the sewing yarn on the inside shoulder edge of the back of your sweater.

4. Insert the needle into the first stitch at the shoulder edge of the front of the sweater. Your needle should have passed under 2 bars and should be on the right side or outside of the work. (Illus. B)

5. Now place the needle under the corresponding stitch of the back of your sweater. (Illus. C) Next your needle will go into the hole that the yarn is coming from on the front and you will go under the next stitch. You will do the same thing on the back now. This is how you continue to weave the sweater together. It is easier if you keep the yarn relatively loose, because

it is easier to see the hole that your yarn is coming from. Pull the sewing yarn tight after you have 6 or 7 stitches and just loosen the last stitch before you proceed.

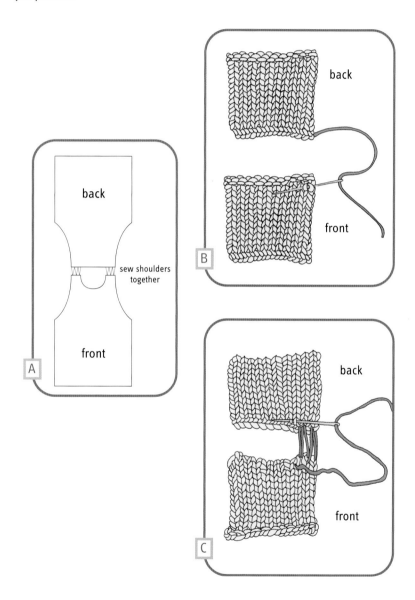

sewing the sleeves to the body

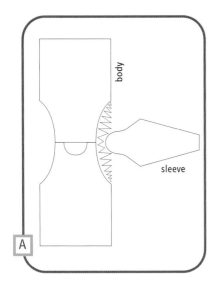

A

This is possibly the most difficult aspect of finishing your sweater, because it is really the only part where something must fit into something else. The cap of your sleeve must fit *perfectly* into your armhole. (Illus. A) That said, sometimes it is possible to fudge it a little to make it work.

1. Cut a piece of yarn approximately 30 inches and thread it through a darning needle.

2. Attach the yarn to the body of the sweater by poking the needle through the edge of the shoulder seam that you made when sewing the shoulders together. Pull the yarn halfway through and make a knot. You should now have half the yarn going down one side of the armhole and half going down the other side.

3. Find the center of the upper sleeve edge by folding the sleeve in half. With the darning needle, pull the yarn under the center 2 bars on the sleeve. (Illus. B) Your sleeve is now attached to the body of the sweater.

4. Now you need to find 2 bars on the body of the sweater. Start at the top near the shoulder seam. This is slightly different from finding the bars on the sleeves because the bars on the sleeves are stitches and on the body, the bars will be rows. Place the needle 1 full stitch in on the body of the sweater and find the 2 bars.

5. Continue sewing as for the shoulders, taking 2 bars from the body and 2 bars from the sleeve and pulling the yarn every few stitches until the sewing yarn is no longer visible and until the sleeve is sewn into the armhole. (Illus. C & D)

B

C

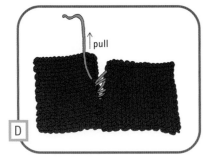

D

sewing side & sleeve seams

1. Cut a piece of yarn approximately twice the length of the sleeve and side seam.

2. Attach the yarn by inserting the sewing needle through the 2 seams at the underarm. Pull the yarn halfway through and make a knot. Half of the yarn should be used to sew the side seam and half should be used to sew the sleeve seam.

3. It doesn't matter whether you start with the body or the sleeve. For both, find the 2 vertical bars 1 full stitch in from the edge and begin the sewing process (Illus. A), taking 2 bars from one side of the sweater and then 2 bars from the other side. (Illus. B) Make sure you are going into the hole where the yarn last came out and pulling the yarn every few stitches. (Illus. C)

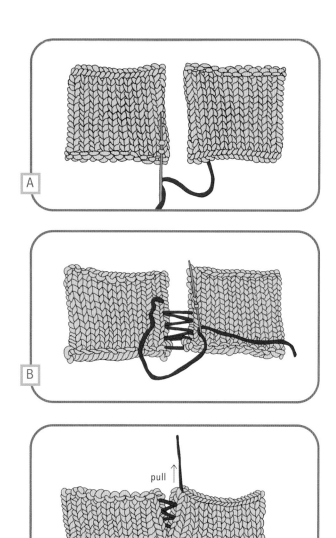

sewing up rolled edges

When sewing up a project that has rolled edges, you will want to finish it so you don't see the seam when the fabric rolls. Start by sewing your seam as you always do, on the right side of the work, BUT at about 1 inch or so before you reach the bottom, you must start sewing on the wrong side of the work instead of the right side. The seam will then show up on the right side, but the rolled edge will cover it.

sewing a raglan sweater together

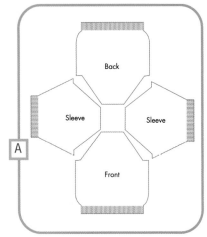

Back

Sleeve

Sleeve

A

Front

Raglan sweaters look intimidating to sew together, but they are actually easier than a set-in sleeve. The sleeve seams always fit perfectly, since you have knit the same number of rows for all the raglan pieces. The easiest way to begin sewing a raglan sweater together is to place all the pieces flat on a smooth surface so the front and back are opposite each other and the sleeves fit into the armholes on opposite sides. (Illus. A) You will sew all the raglan pieces together first. Start at the armhole and sew up to the neck. You will be sewing a sleeve piece to a body piece each time—there will be 4 seams in total here. Once this is done, fold the sweater in half and sew up the side and sleeve seams as you would on a set-in or drop-sleeve sweater.

weaving in ends

While you are knitting, try to keep your ends about 4 inches long. Remember this when you are adding a new ball of yarn or casting on or binding off. If the ends are long enough, you can weave them in with a sewing needle. All you do is thread the needle with an end and weave the yarn back and forth through the seam 3 to 4 times. Then snip the end. You do not need to make a knot. If the ends are too short, you can use a crochet hook.

blocking

Sometimes when a garment is completely assembled, it requires a bit of shaping. Blocking allows you to reshape the piece gently by applying steam, which relaxes the yarn fibers so they can be stretched in order to smooth out bulky seams, even out uneven knitting, or even enlarge a too-small garment.

Not every piece needs to be blocked; use your common sense. But if you decide reshaping or smoothing is in order, pin your garment onto a padded ironing board, easing it into the desired shape. If your iron can emit a strong stream of steam, hold the iron above the piece without touching it and saturate it with steam. Otherwise, dampen a towel, place it over the garment, and press with a warm iron. Allow the piece to remain pinned to the ironing board until it is completely cool.

Never apply a hot iron directly to a knitted piece, and always read the label on your yarn before blocking; some fibers should not be blocked.

picking up stitches

Once the pieces of your sweater are joined, you need to make nice finished edges and button bands. Rather than knit these elements as separate pieces that are then sewn on, we like to knit them directly onto the finished sweater. In order to do this, you must pick up stitches along the finished edges. When you pick up the stitches for a neck, you are generally picking up stitches horizontally in an already-made stitch. When picking up for button bands, you pick up the stitches vertically, in rows. Either way, the method for picking up the stitches is the same; the difference is where you place the needle to pick up the next stitch. You can pick up stitches in existing stitches (vertically, Illus. A–E) or in rows (horizontally, Illus. F–J).

1. Place the work with the right side facing you. Starting at the right edge of your piece with the knitting needle in your right hand, place the needle in the first stitch, poking through from the outside to the inside. (Illus. A & B; F & G)

2. Loop the yarn under and around the needle and pull the needle back through that same stitch. There should be 1 stitch on the needle. (Illus. C & D; H & I)

3. Continue to poke the needle through each stitch, wrapping the yarn around the needle as if you were knitting and adding a stitch to the needle each time. (Illus. E & J)

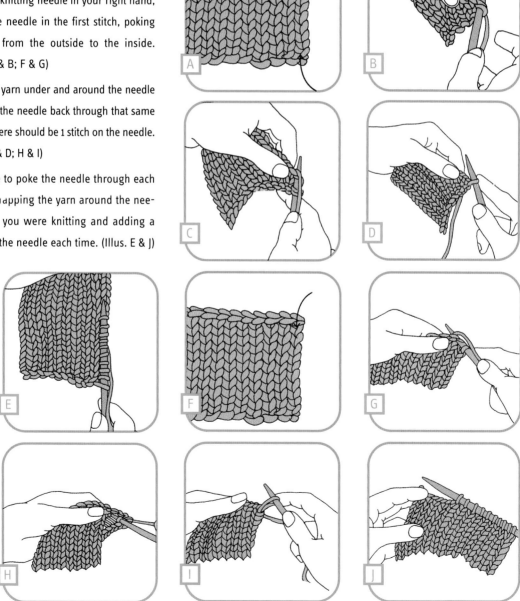

helpful hint

When you are picking up stitches in stitches, as for a crew-neck pullover, most of the time you want to pick up every stitch. It is important to note that there is an extra hole between each stitch. So picking up every stitch is the same thing as picking up every other hole. If you poke your needle through every consecutive hole, you will pick up too many stitches.

When you are picking up stitches in rows, as for a button band, you do not want to pick up a stitch in *every* row. To determine how often to pick up, note your gauge. If your gauge is 3 stitches to the inch, then you will want to pick up stitches in 3 consecutive rows, then skip 1 row and repeat this process. If your gauge is 4 stitches to the inch, you will want to pick up stitches in 4 consecutive rows and then skip 1 row. You must skip a row every so often because there are more rows per inch than stitches per inch. If you were to pick up a stitch in every row, when you started to knit these picked-up stitches, you would have too many stitches and the button bands would look wavy.

RESOURCES

Yarns used in this book can be ordered directly through The Yarn Company. However, yarns change seasonally and it is possible that some of the yarns may not be available when you're ready to place an order. Remember, you do not have to use the exact yarns we used in order to get great results. Just choose a yarn or a combination of yarns that get the required gauge. You can also contact the manufacturer or search online for local retailers. The following is a list of all the distributors whose yarns were used in this book:

THE YARN COMPANY
2274 Broadway
New York, NY 10024
(212) 787-7878/(888) YARNCO1
www.theyarnco.com

ALCHEMY YARNS
P.O. Box 1080
Sebastopolca, CA 95473
(707) 823-3276
www.alchemyyarns.com

BLUE SKY ALPACA YARNS
Blue Sky Alpaca, Inc.
P.O. Box 387
St. Francis, MN 55070
(888) 460-8862
www.blueskyalpacas.com

CRYSTAL PALACE YARNS
Crystal Palace
160 23rd Street
Richmond, CA 94804
(800) 666-7455
www.straw.com

FILATURA DI CROSA, S. CHARLES & TAHKI YARNS
Tahki/Stacy Charles, Inc.
7030 80th Street, Building #36
Floor 1
Glendale, NY 11385
(800) 338-9276
www.tahkistacycharles.com

GGH YARNS & INGEBERG MICHELS
Muench Yarns, Inc.
1323 Scott Street
Petaluma, CA 94954
(800) 733-9276
www.muenchyarns.com

KARABELLA YARNS
Karabella Yarns, Inc.
1201 Broadway
New York, NY 10001
(212) 684-2665
www.karabellayarns.com

KOIGU YARNS
Koigu Wool Designs
563295 Glenelg/Holland Twn Road
RR#1
Williamsford, Ontario NOH2V0
CANADA
(888) 765-WOOL
www.koigu.com

LANG YARNS
Berroco Inc.
14 Elmdale Road
P.O. Box 367
Uxbridge, MA 01569
(508) 278-2527
www.berroco.com

LOUET SALES
808 Commerce Park Drive
Ogdensburg, NY 13669
(613) 925-4502
www.louet.com

ONLINE YARNS
Knitting Fever/Euro Yarns
P.O. Box 502
Roosevelt, NY 11575
(800) 645-3457
www.knittingfever.com

PRISM ARTS INC.
3140 39th Ave. North
St. Petersburg, FL 33714
(727) 528-3800

ROWAN/JAGER YARNS
Westminster Fibers, Inc.
4 Townsend W., Suite 8
Nashua, NH 03063
(800) 445-9276
www.knitrowan.com

INDEX

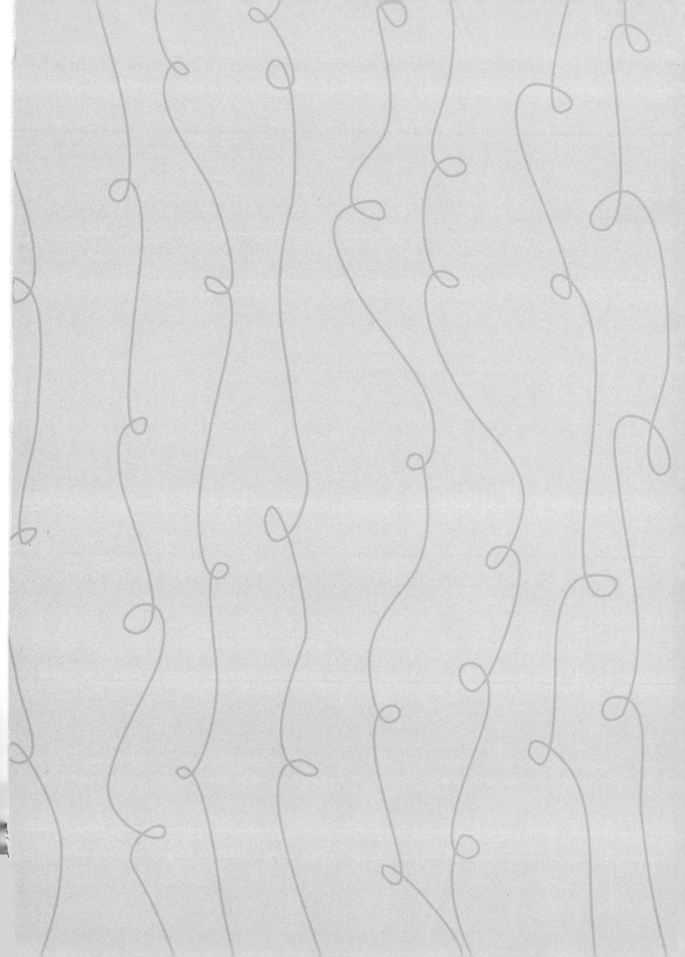